WHY DO CHRI
FIND
TO GRIEVE?

To Jean, Jonathan, Abigail and Daniel.

WHY DO CHRISTIANS FIND IT HARD TO GRIEVE?

Foreword by Richard A. Burridge

Geoff Walters

paternoster
press

First published in the UK 1997 by Paternoster Press

03 02 01 00 99 98 97   7 6 5 4 3 2

Paternoster Press in an imprint of Paternoster Publishing,
P.O. Box 300, Carlisle, Cumbria CA3 0QS

British Library Cataloguing in Publication Data

A catalogue record for this book is available from the British Library.

ISBN 0-85364-787-9

This book is printed using Suffolk Book paper
which is 100% acid free

Typeset by WestKey Ltd., Falmouth
Printed in Great Britain by Clays Ltd., Bungay, Suffolk

CONTENTS

Foreword

One of the great privileges about being involved in Christian ministry is the way one is invited into people's lives at the special moments of existence – joy or sorrow, crisis or decision – the birth of a baby, the love at a wedding, or the death of a loved one. It is at these moments that we are taken out of the day to day routine and we come to the edge of human experience – and, naturally enough, we all ask what we are to make of it, or wonder who we are in such a situation – or who God is, and what is his nature or purpose in it all. At such times, even people of little or no faith turn to a priest or a minister, as a holy person or a sage, to help them to make sense of it all – to seek God's blessing on their love, his care for their child, or his comfort in their grief. Christians, then, ought to be quite good at such special times, and sometimes they are. There is nothing quite like a really good Christian wedding or funeral. And yet, sometimes a funeral seems to ring not quite true, and to be more of a way of avoiding grief. Equally, while many Christians are upheld by their faith in their journey through bereavement, others experience a conflict between their painful feelings and what they consider to be their Christian beliefs. So it is not surprising that many of us involved in taking funerals and caring for the bereaved notice the way faith can appear as both a help and also a hindrance.

As the Chaplain of Exeter University, this was true of my ministry among our staff and students as much as any parish. As also a lecturer in the Theology Department there, I found that such moments of crisis called for theological reflection and study. Such a moment happened when Geoff Walters sent in an essay on bereavement he had written as part of his further training after his ordination as a Baptist minister. Although it was only intended as an initial exploration, its combination of biblical reflection and pastoral care made me realise this too was one of those frontier moments when we were being invited to help make sense of something: why is it that some Christians find it so hard to grieve?

So I began several years of supervising Geoff's research together with my colleague, the Revd Dr Alastair Logan, who specialises in Christine Doctrine and the early church. We were glad to be involved with it, supporting him in the struggle of combining part-time postgraduate study with the demands of a busy ministry. Like all life, it had its moments of birth pangs and difficulties, of love and pain too. Furthermore, Geoff's own personal journey over this time included his own experience of bereavement.

Yet something important was emerging from all the study. The problem with such an immensely wide ranging inter-disciplinary study was that it included different skills and areas, from biblical studies to psychology, from early doctrine and philosophy to modern Christian literature. However, like all the best postgraduate theses, one simple clear argument began to appear: that many Christians' negative views of death and bereavement reflect the idea of the immortality of the soul, which owes more to the philosophy of Plato than the Bible, while the more Christian concept of resurrection in the mercy of God after a real death actually allowed a proper place for grief for the one who has been lost within a context of hope and trust in God. I watched Geoff develop this idea in seminars and his writing, leading eventually to his robust defence of it in the oral examination of his extended thesis. But I also found myself explaining it in my pastoral ministry to people in situations of their grief, and thinking about it again myself when my own mother died. I have used it in my teaching, writing and broadcasting and have been encouraged when others realized that this deceptively simple idea rings true in their experience.

So I am delighted that Dr Walters has drawn upon all that research to produce this book, to enable this idea to reach a wider audience. While his essential argument can be summarised as above in one sentence, it is supported by his research and scholarship over many years and grounded in his pastoral ministry. Now he has made it accessible to many others who will benefit from his work. I am glad to commend it warmly.

The Revd Dr Richard A Burridge
Dean of King's College, London

INTRODUCTION

When I entered the Christian pastoral ministry there was one area of human experience which I expected to encounter which was the source of some anxiety. I was not sure how I would cope with other people's grief. It was not that I had no experience at all of bereavement. I have vague but poignant memories of the impact of the death of my grandfather when I was four. My mother had died several years before my move into the ministry and the strange mixture of confused emotions I had experienced then was still a vivid memory. How could I who, despite a strong Christian faith, did not understand my own feelings at the death of a parent, possibly be of help to those I might encounter grieving the loss of a spouse or a child?

Shortly after my ordination, my senior colleague and mentor, Rev. Ian Burley, went on holiday. Scarcely had he gone, when a man in the church, who had gone into hospital for what we thought was a straightforward operation, died suddenly. He left a widow in her sixties, three married sons and a number of grandchildren. I had no idea what to do. Terrified of saying the wrong thing, I said very little. I gave the family, especially the widow, as much of my time as possible — and I listened to the outpourings of grief and to all the emotional tributaries that flowed into the main stream. When it came to the funeral — my first — I had learned enough about the man and his family to be able to make the service personal and unique to them.

Two things happened during this process which, at the time, surprised me greatly. One was the appreciation of the family and particularly the widow of my inexperienced ministry. Far from being disappointed at my inadequacy and my failure to say 'the right words' she expressed gratitude for the attentive presence of someone who would allow her to say all the things she was feeling. The second surprising thing was my own sense of being at the very heart of pastoral ministry. During those encounters bereavement ceased to be for me a 'morbid' subject and became a door of opportunity to minister the love of Christ authentically. It seemed to me that people in their grief could sometimes come closer to being truly themselves.

Bereavement had become something which interested me. During the months that followed I took a course run by [1]CRUSE, an organisation that exists to support bereaved people, I read a number of books and, of course, I learned most from the many people in bereavement I encountered in the process of pastoral ministry. One or two things were beginning to bother me, however.

To begin with, I noticed that the most helpful wisdom on the subject of bereavement was coming from secular, usually psychological, sources. Christian books, with a few notable exceptions, seemed either to repeat the pronouncements of the psychologists with little or no theological critique or to avoid the real issues facing bereaved people by flight into the next world. Why should this be so? After all, in the Western world the Christian church has had, for centuries, a virtual monopoly on the care of the dying, the disposal of the dead and the support of the bereaved. Was there nothing in our theological tradition which could be applied in an effective way to the care of the grieving today?

Many ministers I had come to know seemed to avoid the issue as much as possible. Bereavement was, for some, a part of the ministry which created discomfort and embarrassment. Some took refuge in liturgical formality, others in doctrinal rigidity. Furthermore, having by now encountered in my work both Christian and non-Christian bereaved people, it started to occur to me that it was often those with a positive and explicit Christian faith who were the 'worst' at grieving or who found grief most embarrassing.

The trigger for the next stage of my thinking was a statement by an elderly Christian widow grieving for her partner of several decades who had died only weeks previously. One evening, when I had responded to a distressed telephone call and gone to see her, she apologized tearfully: 'If I was a *real Christian* I would not get so upset and have to keep wasting your time!' This not untypical comment raises all sorts of questions. Why should this dear lady feel it necessary to apologize for needing the care of her minister following a tragic loss? Why should she think of her perfectly natural grief as inconsistent with her Christian faith? Was there something in Christian belief or in the unconscious set of mind and emotions of Christians which made it difficult to grieve freely? Or was she in fact right? Is grief inappropriate for the Christian? Does it reveal a lack of faith or hope?

It was while I was turning over such questions that my denomination required me to write an extended essay on a pastoral topic of my choice. Naturally I took the opportunity to explore this area further. The title I chose was *The Theology of Bereavement and Its Pastoral Application*. The essay was well received as dealing with a still unexplored but relevant subject and part of it was published as an article in *The Fraternal*, a journal for Baptist ministers. However, I felt the exploration was only just beginning. I was very grateful therefore to the Theology Department of the University of Exeter who agreed to take the subject on as a piece of academic, theological research, and particularly to Drs. Alastair Logan and Richard Burridge who undertook to supervise me on what was still, at this stage, a rather hazy notion.

The original title was long and daunting: *Theological Aspects of the Experience and Suffering of Bereaved People and Their Spiritual Care in the Light of some Contemporary Trends in the Churches*. I suppose our expectation was of an extended version of the original essay. As I proceeded, however, my thinking began to change. The issue of the Christian idea of life after death, which I had so far tended to minimize, became relevant in a new and unexpected way. I began to be interested in the debate about the *way* in which belief in life after death is envisaged in the Christian tradition: the difference between the doctrine of resurrection, rooted in the biblical tradition, and the Platonic concept of the immortality of the soul.

This debate has been going on in theological circles for many years, at least since the publication in 1958 of Oscar Cullmann's revolutionary little book, *Immortality of the Soul or Resurrection of the Dead?* No-one however, to the best of my knowledge, had yet approached the issue from the perspective of the human experience of bereavement. And yet it appeared to me to have an extraordinary relevance.

Here were two models of hope for life after death. One, which could be traced through biblical and intertestamental writings, accepted the fact of death as a reality. It therefore made space for grief: so many biblical characters are depicted as grieving freely. The other, which had its origins in Greek philosophy, particularly the writings of Plato, and found its way into Christian thinking by assimilation during the patristic period, appeared to deny the reality of death. I was struck by the fact that its expression was, from the beginning, so often accompanied by the idea that grief is unworthy of true belief in the afterlife.

Both these models still exist in contemporary Christianity although often in a confused way. Here, I began to feel, was the root of the Christian ambivalence to grief. The *resurrection* model chimes in with contemporary psychological theory which sees grief as suffering and work not to be shirked if the outcome is to be healthy readjustment. The *immortality* model lies at the heart of the discomfort that many Christians feel about grief and the sense that it is unworthy of true faith. If this theory could be demonstrated to be true, it would lead to the striking conclusion that, in this area, what is most biblical is also most therapeutically effective.

This, at least, is what I had come to believe. The focus of my research was sharpened and the title of my thesis shortened to *Resurrection, Immortality and Bereavement*. It was completed and accepted for the degree of Ph.D. at the end of 1993.

Doctoral theses do not necessarily make good reading. Nevertheless, I want to share, perhaps in a more personal and engaged way, some of the things I discovered while doing this research. I believe they will be of help to people like me who are attempting to come alongside grieving people in the context of Christian pastoral care and to the grieving themselves. These ideas may also be of interest to anyone concerned to discover ways in which theology applies to living, contemporary experience. That is my reason for writing this book.

This is not another book on bereavement counselling. There are many such books, both Christian and secular, and some of them are excellent. Although what I am saying has profound implications for the care of the bereaved, this is not the central thrust. This is a book about a theological claim and it is making a point about an important area of Christian belief.

At the same time it is a book written by a practitioner. I did not set out in the first place to write either a thesis or a book but to answer for myself some questions that were presenting themselves to me in the course of my work as a pastor. These questions have led me in an unexpected direction and I submit the conclusions I have come to for the consideration of others who believe, like me, that good theology is, or should be, the soil in which good pastoral practice grows.

PART 1
Grief and the Bible

Chapter 1

GRIEF IN THE OLD TESTAMENT

The old man had reached that point in married life that all couples know to be inevitable but which is seldom anticipated in words or even in personal consciousness. His wife had died. Their marriage had been a long one. It had been passionate, adventurous, turbulent. They had taken risks together. Together they had hoped and despaired, failed and triumphed. There had been times when they had badly let each other down. At times they had clashed violently. They had forgiven and continued to love. Throughout their life together they had trusted God but there had been times when they had both laughed at his promises.

And now it had turned out that it was the old man who was left alone. Perhaps, in his heart of hearts, he had hoped it would be the other way round. Women more often outlive their partners. Perhaps she would have coped with these feelings better than he. She had never been afraid of expressing just how she felt. Of course, he was not alone in an absolute sense. He was a rich and powerful man living in a polygamous society. But no-one would replace this wife of his youth and old age.

His thoughts and feelings were inexpressible to anyone else. There were important and practical things to do. But first, he must see her again. Alone, he went into the innermost part of the tent. Quite possibly, in accordance with the contemporary customs of mourning, his clothes were torn and ashes sprinkled upon his head. Her body lay on an open bier which would soon be laid . . . where? That question could not be put off for much longer in the burning climate but it would have to wait for some minutes — or hours. First the old man knelt by the side of the body of his wife and poured out his heart. His tears fell upon her lifeless form.

And then, when his tears were spent, he got up. He emerged from the tent with all the dignity that everyone who knew him had come to expect. It was time to get on with the business of the moment. Although rich, he was landless, a nomadic chieftain. His wife would not be buried in the sand. There must be a place. Somewhere to return to. A family tomb perhaps, somewhere where he might one day be laid beside the bones of his beloved — and perhaps their descendants after them. But first, it must be a place which would be a worthy enough monument to his love for his wife.

There was a place — a cave at the end of a field owned by a local dignitary among the settled population of the land. The old man made his way to the town and to the place at the gate where a sort of rudimentary town council settled matters of communal importance. The conversation which followed would sound strange to modern Western ears. It seemed as if people were sometimes saying the opposite of what they meant: 'a delightful miniature of adroit oriental conversation',[1] in which hard bargaining took on the disguise of polite flattery and the offering of gifts.

First, the old man explained his predicament. The reply he received was that in view of his importance and riches any of the local landowners would be only too pleased to allow him to place the body of his wife in their tombs. He had only to take his pick. No price was mentioned for the 'rental' at this point. But it was not what he wanted. His beloved would not be placed in another man's tomb. He explained his desire to purchase.

The owner of the field in question stood up. In the presence of all these witnesses he offered his land as a gift. But the old man insisted. He wanted to know the price. The owner in a casual way mentioned the value of the land as a matter of no importance. The field and the cave were a gift. This apparently was considered to be the agreement to a transaction. The 'terms' were accepted and the price paid. The old man was satisfied. He had obtained the only piece of land he had ever owned. His wife of a lifetime had a place to rest. The pain of separation was still in his heart but he had fulfilled for her this final act of love.

Abraham

What you have just read is an interpretation of the account, in Genesis 23, of the reaction of Abraham to the death of his wife, Sarah. It is not the only way in which the words have been interpreted. The facts are that the description of Abraham's grieving is very short and terse (v. 1,2) and the culturally fascinating account of the purchase of the field and cave is quite long and detailed (v. 3–20). It is easy to see why this has sometimes led to a rather cynical reading of the description of Abraham's grief.

The most common contemporary understanding of the chapter is based on the source critical approach to the first five books of the Bible and the Old Testament in general. This approach seeks to identify the authorship and approximate dating of separate sections of the Pentateuch. According to scholars of this persuasion this chapter in Genesis is the work of a writer or group of writers usually referred to as P. P stands for 'priestly'. We are to imagine an author living a millennium and a half after the time of Abraham, during or after the exile of the people of Judah to Babylon. His purpose is to tell the story according to the values of the priests of that time who were anxious to unite and organize the Jewish nation on the basis of law and the observance of a distinctive national religion.

People who believe this to be the background to the chapter tend to see the description of mourning as fulfilling a legal and cultural necessity rather than being an expression of personal grief. The author, it is argued, is not particularly interested in Abraham's grief, which he depicts summarily and in a formalized way — but he does have a much greater interest in Israel's ancestor's claim to ownership of a stake in the land of Canaan.[2]

So, are we reading here a priestly formalist's hasty summarizing of conventional mourning rites followed by more important considerations about land ownership? Or is this a moving account of the profound but dignified grief of an old man on the death of his wife? My own retelling of the story shows where I stand, but I want to stress that this is not an argument about authorship and date but about emotional and psychological content.

Perhaps the simplicity and brevity of this account can be

explained in another way. There is something which critical biblical scholars easily miss but which would be obvious to a modern bereavement counsellor. That is the *normality* of this anecdote of grief. In fact, making allowances for cultural variations, it could easily be a case study in a modern manual on bereavement, illustrating the experience of elderly partners in bereavement:

(1) There is an acute expression of grief in private whereas dignity is maintained in the public domain;
(2) there is a concern to 'do things properly' in terms of the rites of disposal;
(3) there is a desire to do the best for the loved one even beyond death;
(4) there is an acknowledged psychological need for a place of remembrance.

Sarah, like her husband a few years later, died 'old and full of years' (Genesis 25:8). Her death was therefore to be expected, although painful for her husband. One can imagine that he would miss Sarah to the end of his days and yet we would expect Abraham to experience a *normal* and *satisfactory* grief. That is precisely how his bereavement is depicted. Whatever theory of authorship we might adopt concerning Genesis, the fact remains that the account we have of Abraham's grief for his wife is psychologically consistent with the circumstances of her death as we would understand it from the vantage point of the contemporary understanding of grief.

Jacob

Later in the book of Genesis, in chapter 37, we come across another account of grief, this time relating to Abraham's grandson, Jacob. It is a very different sort of narrative and there is nothing about the experience described which could be called normal or satisfactory.

The story comes early in the saga of Jacob's son Joseph. The other ten sons of Jacob have hit on a way to be rid of their irritating younger brother with his arrogant attitude, his pretentious dreams and his highly ornamented or long-sleeved garment marking him out as their father's favourite, the first son of his most beloved wife, Rachel. Joseph has been seized and thrown into a dry cistern. Dissuaded from the ultimate crime of fratricide by the oldest son Reuben (v. 21), the brothers have sold Joseph as a slave to a band of passing Ishmaelite traders.

They now have the embarrassing problem of explaining Joseph's absence to his doting father. The obvious solution is to claim that Joseph has died through no fault of theirs. A goat is slaughtered and the loathed garment stained with the animal's blood. This is presented to the father as proof of his son's death.

In Genesis 37:31–35 we read the reaction of Jacob to the news of his son's death. The fact that Joseph was not really dead and that father and son would, years later, be reunited need not concern us here. To all intents and purposes Jacob is shown as grieving for the death of his son. The stages described are, from the point of view of modern bereavement theory, fascinating.

Firstly, we have the initial reaction to the catastrophic words this father has heard concerning his favourite son. The force of this is not obvious from an English translation. The brothers have just presented the garment to their father and asked, 'We found this. Examine it to see whether it is your son's robe.' Jacob's first words of confirmation are not only a statement of recognition but a repetition of the words he has just heard: 'My son's robe!' In other words, the description of Jacob's reaction at this moment is perfectly consistent with what we would now expect from a person in shock at hearing some terrible and almost unbelievable news — not an answer at all but an uncomprehending, stuttering repetition. Modern bereavement theorists, as we shall later see, would call this the stage of numbness.

This is the first of three climactic sentences in which we observe Jacob attempting to come to terms with what he has just heard. In the words of one commentator: 'These short sentences are extremely dense, mounting in intensity from one to the other and ending with the name Joseph.'[3] The second represents a dawning realisation of what (Jacob supposes) has happened to his son: 'A wild animal has devoured him!' And then, finally, the expression of the horrific implications of what he has seen and heard: 'Joseph is without doubt torn to pieces!' One Jewish commentator points up the realism of what is described: 'The father's exclamations are of great psychological truth and shocking effect.'[4]

What follows next can easily be misunderstood when read from the perspective of modern Western culture: 'Jacob tore his clothes' and 'put on sackcloth'. This sounds like a spontaneous and desperate act, the instantaneous and almost unthinking reaction to grief. Since we will meet these gestures later, it may be as well to say a little about them here. The tearing of garments was throughout the ancient world an accepted response to all kinds of calamities. It is certainly well attested in the Bible. Verses like 2 Samuel 1:11 and Job 1:20 are two typical examples but there are many others. It was, in fact, a custom known through-out the Semitic world and also among the Greeks. Far from always being spontaneous it became so customary that some-times it was a formal and insincere demonstration of grief. In his day, for example, the prophet Joel had to reprimand his people's hypocritical demonstration of grief before God by exclaiming, 'Tear your hearts and not your clothing!' (Joel 2:13).

Similarly the wearing of sackcloth, which to us might seem bizarre and extreme, was an accepted way of publicly demon-strating grief to the outside world. Biblical examples are 2 Kings 6:30 and Amos 8:10 but again these are random examples and there are many others. The custom was also in vogue among Assyrians, Babylonians and other surrounding cultures. It was no more strange than the wearing of black for mourning. It is generally thought to be a symbolic act of renunciation, identifying with the poverty of the dead who now possess nothing.

The point of spelling all this out in the case of Jacob is in no way to insinuate that the writer is depicting Jacob's grief as insincere. It is merely to show that this sentence is a description of Jacob's following the normal and accepted grieving pattern of his day. This is confirmed by the next phrase which tells us that he 'mourned for his son many days.'

It is in the next verse that we begin to see the 'abnormality' of Jacob's grief. One would, of course, both then and now, have expected Jacob to mourn his son for a period of time. One might also reasonably expect that a sadness would remain with him for the rest of his life. However, it might also be expected that Jacob would in time succumb to the comfort of the rest of his family and resume life as normal. This is clearly not to be the case. We can sense a tone of surprise in the narrator's next statement: 'All his sons and daughters *(daughters-in-law?)* came to comfort him but he refused to be comforted.' For Jacob the period of mourning has no foreseeable end.

This is emphasized in Jacob's final exclamation: 'No, in mourning will I go down to the grave to my son.' These words do not mean, as a cursory reading of the English translation might suggest, that Jacob expects to die of grief. Rather, they represent a determination to retain the visible signs of mourning until his dying day. Jacob's grief is unusual not in its intensity but in its extent. Here is a clear example of what modern psychologists would call 'prolonged' or 'chronic' grief.

The sentence with which this episode ends therefore is not about a momentary and instantaneous outburst of tears but a continuous state in which Jacob was to go on living for many years to come. The Jewish commentator Hirsch interprets the verse in a way that is a little imaginative but not at all incongruous: 'When others were merry a furtive tear stole into the eye of the father.'[5]

These verses form a fascinating little cameo of grief, which can be divided into the following stages:

(1) An initial reaction of shock and numbness, giving way to
(2) a gradual realisation of the horror which must be faced;
(3) an acceptance of the customary expressions of public mourning, but
(4) a pathological refusal to bring those expressions to an appropriate close.

Jacob disappears from the story at this point as the emphasis falls on the exploits of his son Joseph in Egypt. It would come as no surprise to a modern bereavement counsellor to find that, when he re-emerges several chapters and many years later, he is still hurt, grieving, insecure and suspicious (Genesis 42:36–38). When his sons return from Egypt reporting that the unknown governor (who is really Joseph) demands to see the youngest son Benjamin, and that Simeon has been left in Egypt as a guarantor, he jumps immediately to the paranoid conclusion that this is all part of a conspiracy against him: 'You have deprived me of my sons. Joseph is no more and Simeon is no more and now you want to take Benjamin. Everything is against me!' It seems unclear whether this suspicion is directed at the remaining sons or at God.

Benjamin is the only full brother to Joseph. He had been born to the favourite wife Rachel as she died. He has become, it would seem, a sort of pathological replacement to Joseph, to be clung to at all costs. The thought of losing Benjamin also would be painful beyond imagination.

As in the case of Abraham, we have read the account of Jacob's grief as a human story, looking at it from the vantage point of a contemporary understanding of bereavement of which the narrator (or narrators) could scarcely have been conscious. What we find shows that the story holds up well against what we currently know about the process of bereavement. This will become clearer still when we look at the modern psychological understanding of bereavement in later chapters.

For this story also, there is a commonly accepted explanation in terms of source critical theory. It is said that while the story of the death of Sarah is written by the later, more formal, priestly writer, P, the account of Jacob's grief is principally the work of an earlier writer known as J because he uses the divine name Yahweh (appearing usually in English translations as 'the LORD' or Jehovah) from the beginning of Genesis.[6] He is said to be a vivid and lively storyteller whose depiction of God is highly anthropomorphic.

This is why, it is argued, we are conscious of so much more feeling in this account. It seems to be the assumption of many commentators that the difference between the calm dignity of Genesis 23 and the raw emotion of chapter 37 can only be accounted for by a difference of authorship. Now, it is not the purpose of this chapter to contest the existence of J and P as separate writers, or to dispute attributions of authorship and date.

The basis of source critical theory has been well argued over the years despite voices of objection raised against it. This book is not meant to be such a voice. Such a hugely influential theory must stand or fall on other grounds. It is a matter of concern, however, if theories of authorship cause us to overlook aspects of the text of Scripture of vital human and spiritual importance and interest.

The striking thing about these passages is that each grief is described in terms totally consistent with the circumstances in which the death is seen to occur. Abraham's grief occured at the end of a long married life. We would expect his grief to be deep but dignified, accepting the inevitable facts of life and death, concerned with providing an appropriate resting place for the person he had loved most in life.

Jacob's grief, on the other hand, involved several complicating factors:

(1) It was the death (he supposed) of his son while still a young man; someone he would not have expected to outlive.
(2) The announcement of the death came without warning; loss was sudden and unexpected.
(3) Death was thought to have occured in a particularly violent and horrifying way.
(4) The loss was that of an already unhealthy and overdependent relationship.

All these factors could be expected to conspire together to create a pathological grief of the kind that, as we shall see, contemporary bereavement theorists might call prolonged or chronic grieving. Whoever wrote the story would be commended by a modern psychologist for his accuracy of human observation.

David

Having begun our examination of the biblical depiction of bereavement in the book of Genesis there are a number of directions in which we might next move. However, the clearest and most vividly realistic accounts of grief in the Old Testament are to be found in the story of the life of David, particularly in the Second Book of Samuel.

Perhaps in this case it would be most helpful to begin by saying something about the classic scholarly analysis of this section of narrative. The story of David is usually thought of as being composed of two blocks of material — usually referred to as the 'History of David's Rise' (1 Samuel 15 — 2 Samuel 5 or 7) and the 'Succession Narrative' (2 Samuel 9 — 1 Kings 2). The accounts of grief I want to examine consist of one story from the first of these blocks and two from the second. The 'Succession Narrative' is usually thought of as having the greater psychological depth and insight, but in both cases we are extremely fortunate to have accounts generally acknowledged as written,

relatively closely to the events described,[7] and with bold frank-
ness. One writer remarks, 'It is indeed a remarkable fact that the
bulk of the Davidic tradition in 2 Samuel relates, not to David's
conquests and imperial administration but to dark episodes in
the history of the royal family.'[8]

How are the mighty fallen!

The first story is told in chapter one of 2 Samuel. It begins with
David and his men in his headquarters at Ziklag, in Philistine
territory. He has narrowly escaped having to fight in the Philistine
army against his own Israelite people under the leadership of
King Saul. The battle had gone badly for the Israelites. Saul, to
whom David is depicted as still showing allegiance despite Saul's
hostility to him, and Saul's son Jonathan, David's intimate friend,
have both been killed.

A man arrives from the battlefield wearing the customary
marks of mourning: his clothes are torn and he has dust or ashes
sprinkled on his head. He brings news of the battle and of the
deaths of Saul and Jonathan. David's ambivalent reaction expresses both shock that such a thing could happen and, at the
same time, eagerness for detail. 'Where have you come from?';
'What happened?'; 'How do you know?' — these are the questions he asks. There are many ways of understanding this
reaction but it is perfectly possible to see it as a normal response
to news of a sudden bereavement. There is shock, disbelief and
an anxious need to verify the facts.

David and his men listen to the full account of the story —
how this messenger had found Saul in the throes of death and
had mercifully ended his life before bringing the crown to David.
In the process, he confesses himself to be an Amalekite, that is
a member of a group detested by the Israelites. It was a raiding
party of Amalekites that David and his men had most recently
annihilated. David's party then fall into what we have seen to be
the expected cultural expressions of grief. They tear their clothes
and spend the rest of the day in weeping and mourning.

What happens next is fascinating when looked at as part of
the process of grieving. David calls for the messenger and,
angrily accusing him of killing 'the Lord's anointed', has him cut
down on the spot. Some commentators apparently find this

incredible.[9] The point at issue is not David's brutality, which can be illustrated from other incidents in his story, but the order and timing of events. It is sometimes assumed that this burst of rage *must* have occurred immediately after hearing the news, not several hours later when David had had time to grieve and to regain his composure. The proposed answer is therefore a displacement of the text. Verses 13–16 should be placed between verses 10 and 11.

This is a wonderful example of the tendency of biblical scholars to assume that every emotional puzzle must have a textual solution. When looked at from a contemporary psychological understanding of bereavement, there is no difficulty at all. Anger is a normal ingredient of the grieving process and is typically directed at those present at the time of death and believed to be in any way responsible. David was simply in a position of power which enabled him to express that anger in a particularly violent way. The point is that, far from coming at a very early stage in the process where we would expect to find — as in this case we did — shock and numbness, anger typically expresses itself later when the fact of death has been assimilated. The order of events is perfectly psychologically credible.

The rest of chapter one is in poetic form. What we find here is a typical and very beautiful example of a *qinah* or lamentation song.[10] This particular genre of Hebrew poetry is common in the Old Testament. Later its use was extended from the expression of personal grief to giving vent to national or political feeling. Its most developed form is in the book of Lamentations. One of the characteristics of this form is the repetition of phrases beginning with the exclamation '*How . . . !*' In this case the phrase '*How the mighty have fallen!*' comes at the beginning, in the main body and at the end of the poem.

David begins by expressing the shame of Israel in defeat and then imagines the scene of the disaster, invoking a sort of curse upon it. Then he embarks upon what has been called a 'panegyric of Saul and Jonathan'.[11] This (v. 23–26) is a remarkable and beautiful passage. David's friendship with Jonathan is proverbial and there is no surprise in the outburst of personal emotion expressed for him — even if the language is, to Western ears, somewhat extreme. What is fascinating about this poem, however, is that it contains no hint of the long history of animosity between Saul and David. On the contrary, Saul is praised in almost equally extravagant terms.

Logically, one might suspect David of insincerity and yet the tone of the poem belies this. Many commentators remark on the apparent genuineness of emotion shown here[12] and it has even been argued that the anomaly works in favour of the argument for genuine Davidic authorship since 'an imitator would have included something' of the discord of the previous relationship.[13] Anyone who has heard a bereaved person idealize their far from ideal loved ones will recognize what is happening here.

It is perhaps worth pointing out at this juncture something which may come as a great surprise to many readers of the Bible. It is something true not only of this picture of grief but also of those we have already observed and those which will follow. Although we see here a great depth of human emotion in grief, there is no attempt whatever to find or provide comfort through religious belief.

It might be assumed that the reason for this is the Old Testament's rather negative view of death. We shall see later that although some Old Testament passages speak of the dead existing in Sheol, this is for the most part seen as a very shadowy and negative form of existence. Only in later Old Testament passages does a clearer and more positive hope emerge. It could be argued that this is why there is a striking absence of religious comfort for bereavement in passages such as these.

Nevertheless, one might have expected Yahweh's covenant relationship with his people to have provided some acknowledgeable support at such a time, particularly when recounting the story of David. After all, David's personal election by and relationship with God is something that the writer or writers of these narratives are particularly eager for their readers to understand. Nevertheless, God is not mentioned in this *qinah* or in the narrative in which it is set. The striking implication of this is that David, God's chosen one, like Abraham and Jacob whom we have already observed, faces grief in its full pain without any attempt at mitigation by finding support in the love of God!

Before leaving this extremely full account of Israel's great hero in bereavement, it is worth cataloguing the aspects of David's grief that are recorded:

(1) Shocked disbelief on hearing the news of death;
(2) An expression of grief, once the news of death had been assimilated;
(3) Violent blame of those present at the death and held responsible;
(4) Anguished visualisation of the scene of death;
(5) Idealized praise of the deceased;
(6) An outpouring of intimate, personal feelings;
(7) A refusal to find comfort even in cherished beliefs.

This is perhaps the most detailed account of a personal grief in the Bible and it is fascinating to find in it so many features which are common to the human experience of grief in the modern world, as indeed in all ages.

Is the child dead?

We find David experiencing grief again at a much later point in his story. The account is in 2 Samuel 12. We have passed possibly into the hands of a different author, the writer of the 'Succession Narrative' or 'Court History' of King David. If there is any change in tone, it is that the psychological detail becomes even more intense.

David now reigns as king over all Israel and an empire of surrounding states from his newly conquered capital of Jerusalem. However, he has been exposed by the prophet Nathan for his adultery with Bathsheba and his complicity in the death of her husband Uriah. Their child is seriously ill and David believes that its impending death is a judgement upon himself. He is nevertheless deeply in love with Bathsheba and longs for her child to survive.

The narrative tells us that while the child is ill David puts himself through some characteristic expressions of grief: he fasts and lies on the ground. Some manuscripts add that he lay 'in sackcloth'.[14] When the baby eventually dies, his courtiers are, not surprisingly, afraid to give him the news of the child's death in case he does 'something desperate' (v. 18, NIV). When he hears the news, however, he washes, anoints himself, puts on fresh clothes and eats food, all actions which were forbidden in mourning.[15]

This is a puzzling story and it has often been questioned

whether David is really mourning at all for this baby or whether he is merely humbling himself in penitence and begging God to spare the child's life. David's actions, however, are all characteristic of grief. It seems that David is grieving in anticipation of the death of his son and that, when the death occurs, he is able to face it with equanimity.

The concept of anticipatory grief is a controversial one and it is admittedly rare for someone to have completed the process of grieving by the time that a death takes place. These circumstances are, however, to say the least, unusual and it might be more accurate to say that, although David stops publicly mourning the death of his son, his private grieving is not over. Certainly, David's final words on the subject indicate that his sadness persists: 'I will go to him but he will not return to me' (v. 23).

In view of what was said earlier about the lack of religious comfort in grief in these stories, it is interesting to note here that the worship of God, along with washing and eating, is something that David allows himself once the expression of grief is over (v. 20). It is not unusual for even the most devout of people to find customary habits of worship difficult to maintain when in the pangs of acute grief.

Absalom, my son, my son!

The third picture of David in grief comes at a yet further stage in his career. It is described in 2 Samuel 18:31–19:8. Late in life the kingdom is almost torn from his hand by the rebellion of his son, Absalom. Before the final battle between the armies of father and son, David had given the contradictory and almost impossible order that his son is not to be harmed. It is David's men who win the day, thus regaining the kingdom for him. In the aftermath of the battle David's chief general, his nephew Joab, ensures the death of Absalom. But how is the king to be informed?

The exquisite narrative skill of the writer of this part of David's story is shown in the build-up of tension towards the breaking of the news. The wily Joab, remembering perhaps what had happened to the Amalekite, ensures that it is a foreign mercenary and not the priest's son, Ahimaaz, who, believing himself the bearer of glad news of victory, tells the king, in as gentle a way as possible, of the death of Absalom. In this case, however, the period of numbed shock is too intense and too extended, for David to be seen responding in anger. David, overcome with the news he has heard, retreats into a private room, repeating his son's name: 'O my son, Absalom! My son, my son, Absalom! If only I had died instead of you — O Absalom my son, my son!' (18:33).

There is no doubt that an angry reaction is feared. There is a vivid picture of the victorious army creeping back into the city as if they had fled in defeat. David however is totally absorbed in the news of what he had feared and perhaps half-expected. He withdraws further into private grief as he covers his face and goes on aimlessly repeating his son's name. The hard-headed Joab, however, 'machine-guns the king with words'[16] and insists that David go and speak to his disillusioned men before the victory turns against him and he ends up in a worse political situation than before.

The Dutch commentator, J.P. Fokelmann, offers an interesting psychological interpretation of what is going on. He describes a 'dualistic mentality' in David who 'should have realized that he could not retain both the throne and the son. Retention of one really presupposes the loss of the other.' David, however, makes an almost masochistic choice of the suffering of grief rather than the joy of regaining the throne. 'The dualism of the ego then guarantees that David will split off precisely that half of the reality which can bring him fortune . . . and be engulfed by the other half, suffering for Absalom.' Even though David obeys Joab and, just in time, regains his grip on the people's loyalty, his 'position is still ambivalent: in the foreground is the meaning that he is thinking of his throne and wishes to be with the soldiers as the king, but in the background the pain and grief loom large as life'.[17] What we have here is an amazingly accurate description of real but pathological grief which, we may suppose, will shadow the rest of David's life.

In these cameo accounts of personal bereavement from the Old Testament we have observed a number of features which it may be helpful to summarize:

(1) In all of the stories, written by a variety of authors at different times and in different political and religious contexts, the reality

of grief is fully acknowledged. The need to grieve is never denied.
(2) The features of grief described chime with the findings of
the modern psychological study of bereavement. All the accounts
are perfectly psychologically credible. This will become more
apparent when, later in the book, we examine some of these
findings.
(3) Although it has been traditional among biblical scholars to
account for differences in details in the narratives in terms of
textual theories, these differences can just as easily be attributed
to differences in the circumstances and personalities of the
protagonists. A number of 'puzzles' disappear when they are
read as human stories.
(4) It is perhaps startling to discover that, although the people
concerned are otherwise depicted by the authors as having great
religious sensibilities, at no time are their religious beliefs or
personal faith in God seen as modifying or even bringing comfort
in the experience of grief.

These considerations are, I believe, of great importance to the
discussion of the experience of grief among Christians today. It
may be thought, however, that much of what has been said can
be attributed to the somewhat hazy or even negative attitudes
sometimes expressed in the Old Testament towards death and
the belief in life after death. Surely the clarity of teaching about
resurrection and the hope of eternal life in the New Testament
should, for Christians today, transform the experience of bereavement! To see whether such an expectation holds water, we
shall, in the next chapter, examine some New Testament descriptions of grief.

Chapter 2

GRIEF IN THE NEW TESTAMENT

News was beginning to spread around Galilee about the violent death of John the Baptist. Pious and patriotic Jews were enraged. Not only had the ruler of the region, Herod Antipas, had John beheaded without trial, he had done so, it was being said, on a whim — as a promise to a girl, the daughter of his illegal wife Herodias, whose dancing had caught his eye at his birthday party. Emotions were running high.

One of the few people not yet to have heard the news was the Rabbi Jesus of Nazareth. Jesus had sent his band of twelve disciples out into the surrounding towns and villages and was awaiting their return with news of their exploits. Two by two they trickled back, full of stories of what they had said and done and the impact of their mission. One of the final pair reported: 'Everyone is talking about you, Master. Some say you are Elijah or one of the prophets come back to life. And old Herod is really worried. he thinks you are John the Baptist whom he had beheaded!' Laughter spread around the group but quickly subsided. Everyone was looking at Jesus' face. 'Oh, Master didn't you know that John was dead?' The story was quickly told.

Jesus, usually the animating force in their lively conversations, had gone quiet. An unusual bond had united the lives of the two men. They were closely related and close in age. Stories of miraculous happenings surrounded both their births. No-one was very sure how much contact there had been between the two boys as they grew up because neither had spoken much about it, but it had been John, the first of the two to achieve fame, who had pointed Jesus out to the crowds and said that this man was so much greater than he that he was not worthy to untie the thongs of his sandals.

But Jesus did not speak about what he was feeling. 'Crowds are beginning to gather,' he finally said, 'We all need some time alone to rest. Get the boats ready and let's get across the lake to Bethsaida.' The proposed quiet retreat was not to be, however. Before the boat landed people were already gathering on the shore. Another day of teaching lay ahead. The stage was being set for the story of the miraculous feeding of over five thousand people.

Jesus and John

Of course, you will not read precisely that story in any of the four gospels! It is a possible but slightly imaginative conflation of the stories found in Matthew, Mark and Luke. Mark and Luke place in immediate proximity the sending out and return of the twelve, reference to the beheading of John the Baptist, the withdrawal of Jesus and his disciples to a quiet place and the subsequent feeding of the five thousand. Matthew has a similar order but omits reference to the disciples' mission.

It is Matthew's account, in fact, which holds interest for the subject of bereavement. Matthew says that Jesus decided to withdraw 'when (he) heard what had happened' (NIV). The tense of the verb suggests the interpretation 'immediately upon hearing'. The context makes it clear that it is hearing about the death of John that caused Jesus to want to withdraw. In fact the disciples are not mentioned until the arrival on the other shore. Rather, Matthew says '. . . he withdrew by boat privately to a solitary place'. Although it is obvious that Matthew acknowledged the presence of the disciples, his emphasis is upon Jesus' personal feelings.

Now, we know that a common reaction of a bereaved person is to want to withdraw from a public to a private place — to be alone, or at least with people close enough to be trusted. We have seen it in the story of Abraham and Sarah and that of David and Absalom. It is well attested in psychological literature on bereavement and no doubt many readers of this book will have experienced it or seen it in their friends. It is therefore natural to suppose that Matthew here is giving us a brief but clear picture of Jesus in grief. I have to report, however, that I have yet to find a commentary on the Gospel of Matthew which takes this as the natural interpretation.

Instead, it is practically universal to assume that Matthew shows us Jesus retreating at this point *to avoid a confrontation with Herod!*[1] Typically, one quite recent commentator asks us to: 'Note also that because the motive for withdrawal has become John's execution, the reader no longer thinks of Jesus and his disciples as seeking rest in a spiritual corner; they rather are going into hiding.'[2] Of course, it is embarrassing to think of Jesus as being afraid, so it is often suggested that Jesus did not want to cause a political stir at this early stage of his ministry and was merely avoiding trouble for the time being.[3]

This motive, even if feasible given the personality of Jesus, is quite different to that recorded by Mark, followed closely by Luke — that Jesus and his disciples withdrew for a rest following their hectic mission. An opposition is immediately set up between Mark and Luke on the one hand and Matthew on the other. Little wonder then that, given a choice between a Jesus going into hiding and a Jesus caring for the physical and spiritual well-being of his followers, the latter is thought to be preferable.[4] Mark wins over Matthew!

Such an opposition is unnecessary, however, if the much more natural interpretation of a grief reaction is assumed. A fleeing Jesus does not have to be explained away and a harmony between the three accounts in something like the form I have imagined is easily possible: the needs of a grief-stricken Jesus and twelve road-weary and emotionally exhausted disciples co-incide. They need quiet and rest.

My point, however, is not the harmonisation of the synoptic gospels. I am fascinated by the question of *why* the idea of Jesus in grief should be so studiously avoided. We have seen that grief in the Old Testament is a fact of life. In the New Testament, it seems to be assumed that a different attitude should prevail — particularly when looking at Jesus. It is my view that what is at work here in the minds of commentators, as indeed in the minds of many Christians, is an unconscious form of docetism: the heresy that denies the real humanity of Jesus. It seems that only so much human emotion can be allowed to be seen in Jesus. The line is drawn at the idea of Jesus grieving, simply and naturally, for the death of a beloved relative and friend.

Jesus Wept

We see the strength of this docetism even more clearly — and perhaps begin to glimpse the reasons for it — in the common interpretations of another account of Jesus in grief, this time in John's Gospel: the story of the raising of Lazarus in John, chapter 11. In this story, John shows us Jesus deliberately arriving at the home of his friends, Martha, Mary and Lazarus in Bethany, four days after Lazarus' death. He had already said to his disciples, 'Our friend Lazarus has fallen asleep, but I am going there to wake him up' and then affirmed plainly, 'Lazarus is dead' (v. 14).

On arrival in Bethany he is met by the grieving sisters, one at a time. With Martha, the first, he engages in conversation about resurrection and makes the stunning statement: 'I am the resurrection and the life. He who believes in me will live, even though he dies' (v. 25). He is taken by the wailing villagers to the cave-tomb where Lazarus's body has been laid and there ensues the miracle of the raising of Lazarus from the dead. This miracle is not to be seen as a 'resurrection' in the sense of the resurrection of Jesus. There is no indication that the raised body of Lazarus has the property of immortality. Rather the miracle seems to be recorded to demonstrate Jesus' power over death itself and serves as a powerful symbol of the resurrection both of Jesus and of those who have faith in him.

What is of principal interest here, however, is the depiction of Jesus' emotions as he approaches the resting place of his friend. The NIV translates the relevant passage like this:

> When Jesus saw her (Mary) weeping, and the Jews who had come along with her also weeping, he was deeply moved in spirit and troubled. 'Where have you laid him?' he asked.
> 'Come and see, Lord,' they replied.
> Jesus wept.
> Then the Jews said, 'See how he loved him!'
> (v. 33–36).

The language used in this rare cameo of Jesus' feelings is extremely graphic and vivid. For instance, the word used in the striking phrase, 'Jesus wept', is a different one from that used to describe the weeping of the other mourners which, while not implying any insincerity, could easily be translated 'to wail'. The verb used of Jesus, however, is derived from the word for 'a tear'. This fact, combined with the aorist tense, suggesting a single, rather than continuous action, makes it perfectly legitimate to translate the phrase, 'Jesus burst into tears'. It seems hard to avoid the image of Jesus in emotional turmoil.

This is further emphasized by the word translated 'troubled' meaning 'disturbed' or 'agitated'. There is a tradition which attempts to play down the impact of this verb by stressing that it is a reflexive form: 'he troubled himself'. Later in this book, we shall have cause to note the attitude of St. Augustine to Christian grief. At this point it is interesting to note his comment on this phrase. 'You will be troubled unwillingly,' he notes, 'Christ is troubled because he wills it.'[5] The tradition of Augustine's refusal of a Jesus at the mercy of human emotion is well represented by this statement from a modern commentary: 'Christ's affections were . . . orderly, rational, full of dignity and directed to proper ends.'(!)[6] Such docetism, however, is totally unjustified on the basis of this phrase. John frequently uses the reflexive form in a passive sense and the most natural translation is simply that Jesus was troubled.

So far, there would seem to be nothing in the words used to indicate that Jesus was suffering anything other than grief for a dead friend. Certainly, that was the assumption of the bystanders who said, 'See how he loved him!' Controversy, however, surrounds one word, ambiguously translated 'deeply moved' by the NIV. It is used in verse 33 together with the phrase 'in his spirit' and again in verse 38, where Jesus arrives at the tomb, in conjunction with the phrase 'in himself'.

This is an extremely picturesque word which derives from the snorting noise made by a horse! The accompanying phrases however indicate that this was an internal emotion rather than a noise that Jesus made. It is clearly a metaphorical image — but what does it indicate? On the other three occasions when this verb is used in the New Testament (Matthew 9:30; Mark 1:43; Mark 14:5) it relates to stern warnings or indignant anger. One line of argument therefore stresses that Jesus must have been angry.[7] Opinion in this school of thought divides into two camps: those who believe he was angry at the unbelief or hypocrisy of the mourners around him, and others who think his anger was directed at the spiritual forces of evil and death which seemed to have the upper hand at this point. Others claim that it is not possible to be dogmatic about the precise meaning of a metaphorical phrase such as this. They would say that its meaning must be governed by other words in the immediate context which, as we have seen, clearly indicate grief.[8]

So, biblical scholars debate whether Jesus is here expressing anger *or* grief. The very existence of the debate would bring a wry smile to the face of a bereavement psychologist. Anger and grief are not contradictory emotions. One is in fact a component of the other. We have learned from David, if nowhere else, that grief encompasses anger. Jesus had known for four days that Lazarus was dead. He had had a long walk in which to absorb this information. We shall see later, in Part 4 of this book, that there is nothing more emotionally normal than that Jesus should be feeling angry. The object of his anger is hardly relevant. All sides of the interpretative argument are both right and wrong!

The question remains, however: *why* is there this massive reluctance on the part of so many Christians, including biblical scholars, to accept a grieving Jesus? The answer, I believe, lies beyond textual arguments. This passage of John's Gospel, it will be remembered, is concerned with resurrection. It contains the most explicit teaching on resurrection and climaxes with a story of a raising of the dead. What appears to be paradoxical is that the same chapter also contains vivid language depicting grief in the person who not only has the power to raise the dead but is described as Resurrection and Life. The question the passage poses therefore is: can grief co-exist with belief in resurrection? Those who would deny this *a priori* have no choice but to play down the language of grief or to try to make the words mean something else. One commentator for instance believes that we are receiving here: 'a lesson not to mourn for the dead as those without hope'.[9] To take with equal seriousness both aspects of the passage — both the grief and the glory — turns this argument on its head. We find the evangelist teaching us the surprising reality that grief is a valid response to death, even for those who hope for resurrection beyond death.

The debate here is rooted in Christology and related to our view of the intentions of the Fourth Evangelist. For many years

Johanine studies have been dominated by the views of Ernst Käsemann who saw any traces of human characteristics in John's depiction of Jesus as 'the absolute minimum of the costume designed for the one who dwelt for a little while among men'.[10] I believe this is to seriously miss the point. If John stresses the divinity of Christ more emphatically than the synoptic authors, it is no less true that he is concerned with the Word who 'became flesh'. Jesus is not shown as condescendingly pretending to grieve in an act of sympathy with our weaknesses but as really grieving — as both man and God — precisely at that point where resurrection is demonstrated most powerfully. Perhaps we shall later get a clearer glimpse of why this is so.

Grief on the Road to Emmaus

So much for the grief of Jesus. What about the grief of New Testament Christians? The most obvious place to start is to look at the depiction of the response of Jesus' disciples to the crucifixion. The fact that their grief was short-lived does not detract from its reality. Perhaps the most vivid description is to be found in the story of the two disciples on the road to Emmaus in Luke 24:13–27. We shall see later that the modern study of bereavement began in the medical discipline of psychiatry. In New Testament times it is interesting that it is Luke the 'physician' who gives us this most detailed and well-observed picture of two people in grief. Their identity need not concern us here.[11]

Firstly we find them talking in detail about the events leading up to and surrounding the death of Jesus. This thirst for detail is typical of the early stages of bereavement. The verb translated 'discussed' (literally they 'sought together' or debated) suggests that they were not in complete agreement. They can be seen therefore as trying to put the chaotic events of the last few days into some kind of order.

At this point the risen Jesus approaches them. The reason for their non-recognition of Jesus need not concern us, although it is possible that their grief-stricken mental state played some part. Whatever the reason, they react to the interruption by 'standing still with downcast faces'. Although they had been speaking freely to each other, they find it difficult to share their feelings with a stranger. Instead they adopt the depressed appearance we associate with the phase of grief in which the reality of loss has finally sunk in.

Jesus shows himself to be an excellent bereavement counsellor. He does not reveal himself straight away — that would be to deny their grief before they had fully had chance to accept it — but gives them opportunity to talk through their feelings. He asks simple, open-ended questions and then listens while they pour out their story. Only then does he begin to instruct them, still without revealing his identity.

During this outpouring an interesting element of their grief emerges. 'But we had hoped,' they say, 'that he was the one who was going to redeem Israel.' An important aspect of bereavement is the acceptance of unfulfilled expectations. Bereaved people suffer the loss of what might have been: watching a child grow, for example, or a happy retirement together. For the disciples their expectation of a renewed kingdom of Israel had been crushed. Indeed, it was never going to happen just as they had hoped. This was a real loss with which they had to come to terms.

Whatever Luke's sources for this story he shows himself, as elsewhere, to be an excellent observer and recorder of human detail. Here, almost incidentally, he gives us a portrayal of people in grief which is accurate even in terms of modern clinical understanding. It could still be argued, however, that this is still the grief of people who do not yet know about resurrection.

Grief in Jerusalem

The first recorded Christian death after the crucifixion of Jesus is that of the martyr, Stephen. As we read his story we are once again in the hands of that acute observer of human life, Doctor Luke, this time in his sequel to the story of Jesus, the Book of Acts. Two things stand out in the narrative of the stoning of Stephen (Acts 7:54–8:1). The first is the obvious parallel which Luke draws with the death of Jesus. Stephen, like Jesus, prays for the forgiveness of his murderers and, as Jesus committed his 'spirit' to the Father, so Stephen commits his to the Lord Jesus. The second striking thing is Stephen's vision of Jesus, standing to receive him in heaven. There would seem little doubt that Luke wants to assure us of Stephen's eternal destiny. Here is a man who dies like his master and who will surely, like him, be raised from the dead to enjoy eternity in the presence of God.

It is of great interest, therefore, to observe the recorded reaction of Stephen's fellow Christians to this paradigmatic death. Luke sums this up simply in one sentence: 'Godly men buried Stephen and mourned greatly for him' (Acts 8:2). The word used for 'mourning' here originates from the verb 'to beat' and suggests a beating of the chest in grief. This combined with the word 'great' suggests an outpouring of deep emotion. So, in the very earliest days of the church's life, Christians are seen grieving for the death of one of their number despite the firmest assurances of his eternal welfare.

Perhaps after what we have seen already, it will come as little surprise to discover that the majority of scholarly comment avoids this conclusion — or indeed vehemently denies it. It cannot be denied, of course, that Luke intends to show us mourning taking place. What comes into question is who it is that is doing the mourning. Most commentators deny that these 'godly men' were in fact Christians. One old and much followed commentary stated starkly that 'S. Stephen lacked Christian burial'.[12]

Two reasons are given for this conclusion. One is that the term 'godly men' itself suggests that the mourners were Jews.[13] They could hardly be otherwise given the context in Jerusalem at this time, but the inference being drawn is that they were non-Christian Jews. The same word is used later, however, to describe the disciple Ananias in Damascus who is, no doubt, a Jewish convert to the Way of Jesus (Acts 22:12). The word can, therefore, be said to apply to Christian Jews also.

The second reason given is that Christians would have been putting themselves too much at risk by holding a public funeral for one of their leaders.[14] The weakness of this argument is shown by the fact that any such mourning would have been a risky business, whoever was doing it. The Rabbinic teaching of the Mishna forbade any public show of lamentation at the burial of an executed criminal (Sanh. 6:6). The only mourning permitted was that which 'has place in the heart alone'.

Whoever mourned greatly for Stephen was going out on a limb. They were 'in effect mounting a public protest against the execution of Stephen'.[15] Is it really likely that non-Christian rather than Christian Jews would be mounting such a protest? Luke portrays a Jerusalem fairly well polarized by the Jesus issue at this point. There is no hint of a neutral and fair-minded section of the population who would have wanted to do right by Stephen while rejecting his beliefs.

The most natural reading of this verse is that the members of the first Christian church, while no doubt deriving some comfort from Stephen's dying words, nevertheless were deeply grieved at his death and were courageous enough to put their own lives at risk by a public display of their grief. It is hard to escape the conclusion that the real reason for the almost wholesale rejection of this obvious understanding is more subtle than the reasons stated.

In the Book of Acts, and particularly in its early chapters, we read about the church in the first flush of its Spirit-inspired power and energy. Despite the persecution and the difficulties being encountered, the tone is one of victory. Death has been conquered and resurrection is assured to those who believe in Jesus. In this highly-charged spiritual atmosphere, it is perhaps difficult to imagine that grief has a place; that the breast-beating pains of grief are the appropriate emotions for Christians when one of their number takes his place beside the Saviour in heaven. This, however, is precisely the conclusion to which these few words from Luke seem to point us. It is easy to see why ordinary Christians as well as learned commentators miss the point of this verse.

Grief in Thessalonica

Someone had died in the small, new Christian church at Thessalonica. The event had caused consternation and anguish. The natural grief of these Christians at losing someone they loved was compounded by a theological problem. On their understanding of Christian teaching, this should not have happened! It had been only months since they had heard from Paul and his companions the 'good news' about Jesus and had formed themselves into this new kind of community. They had learned about eternal life for believers and about the ushering in of a new age when the risen Jesus would return in power. But strong opposition from the Jewish community in Thessalonica had forced the missionaries to move on and these young Christians had been left to make what they could of the elements of Christian teaching which they had been able to remember.

The death of one of their members came as a complete shock. Did this mean that their loved one had missed the *parousia*, the 'appearing' of Jesus? Would this person be lost for ever? Who else might die before 'the Day' came? Did such an event cast doubt on all that Paul had taught them?

Paul meanwhile had moved on to Beroea where it seemed as if his mission was encountering greater success than in Thessalonica until some of the Thessalonian Jews arrived on the scene to stir up trouble. Once again he would have to move on. But where? He longed to go back to Thessalonica. He was aware that he had left the few Christians there in a difficult and vulnerable predicament. How would they cope with the opposition they encountered? Would they have the courage to bear witness openly to their faith? What gaps had he left in the essential teaching they needed to avoid manipulation by the arguments of his opponents? More than that, in the short time he had known them he had come to love them. He had been 'torn away' from them too soon (1 Thessalonians 2:17).

However, a return to Thessalonica was, for the time being, impossible. He must move on to Athens to face a different kind of challenge. But so great was his anxiety that he sent his friend and 'apprentice' Timothy back to Thessalonica to see how things were. Timothy could not have been more delighted at what he found. He was able to bring back to Paul a most encouraging report of the Thessalonians' progress in faith and witness, and also a catalogue of questions clustering around the issue of their grief. It was in answer to this report and these questions that Paul wrote what may be the earliest extant piece of Christian literature, now known as the First Letter to the Thessalonians.

Paul, a model pastor as well as a missionary-evangelist, fills his letter with encouragement. He demonstrates to his readers that he too understands the pain of separation from loved ones (2:17–20). He gives them practical advice on Christian living. Not until he is three-quarters of the way through his letter does he come to the Thessalonians' big problem. Now he knows the major missing ingredient in the Thessalonian Christians' understanding of Christian theology: it is the doctrine of resurrection. Whether he had omitted to teach it or they had forgotten it is immaterial. This is the piece of the jigsaw puzzle which will complete their picture.

> We believe that Jesus died and rose again and so we believe that God will bring with Jesus those who have fallen asleep in him (4:14).

This means that they have no cause to be anxious about their members who are already dead. When Jesus appears, those who are still alive at the time will have no advantage. 'The dead in Christ will rise first!' All of us, without exception will be in the Lord's presence for ever. This, he informs them, is grounds for mutual encouragement.

The matter is dealt with simply and without fuss. They are not to concern themselves about *when* all this is to happen. This is God's surprise — a pleasant surprise for people like them who are 'in the light'. They are to reassure themselves and get on with the business of Christian living.

In introducing this subject, however, Paul uses a sentence which, taken out of the context of the Thessalonian predicament has been interpreted in a way designed to play havoc with the Christian view of grief. Here it is:

> Brothers, we do not want you to be ignorant about those who fall asleep, or to grieve like the rest of men who have no hope (4:13).

What is Paul saying here? Is he forbidding Christians to grieve? Does he insinuate that grief itself is only appropriate to those who are without hope? This is precisely the way that Paul's words have often been understood. An old but very influential commentary states that Paul 'does not mean that the Christians are indeed to grieve but not in the same manner or degree as the unbelievers . . . Paul speaks absolutely . . . In view of this glorious consummation, present grief, however natural, is excluded.'[16] This point of view has been followed by many later commentators.[17] It is, however, an extremely unlikely reading of Paul's words.

To begin with, it would be hard to reconcile such an understanding with statements made by Paul elsewhere concerning the natural human response of grief. We have seen that even in this letter he demonstrates the pain he feels at being separated from people he has come to love. Elsewhere, he is more specific. In his letter to the Romans, for example he calls on Christians to

'Rejoice with those who rejoice and mourn with those who mourn' (Romans 12:15). The word used is the same as that which describes the kind of wailing going on at the tomb of Lazarus. Paul seems here to be asking Christians to identify with each other's public grief.

An even more striking example of Paul's real attitude to grief comes in his letter to the Philippians. He is speaking to the Philippian Christians about one of their number, Epaphroditus who had been with him but who had become dangerously ill. He had feared for Epaphroditus's life but had been grateful to God who had spared his life 'so that I might not have grief upon grief' (Philippians 2:27). The word 'grief' is the same as that used in Thessalonians. Here Paul confesses himself capable of the experience of grief — he would have experienced terrible grief if Epaphroditus had died.

Given examples like these it is hard to imagine Paul putting an absolute prohibition upon grief for Christians. But this, of course, is not what he is doing. He says that the Thessalonians are not to grieve 'just like' the others. He uses a strong expression meaning 'in exactly the same way'. There is an element here which makes Christian grief distinctive. It is the element of hope. The mistake often made is to assume that hope in some way cancels out grief. Paul does not say this. Indeed a closer look at Paul's theology, as expressed say in Romans 8, would show that while he may speak of hope as present in human suffering, he never expects it to eradicate the suffering. Instead it is to be seen as a resource for coping.

So, in this instance, Paul brings the element of hope into the grief of the Thessalonian Christians precisely because their grief is real. This is confirmed a few verses later when he says 'comfort one another with these words'. He uses the classic New Testament word for comfort which means 'calling alongside'. It is Jesus' word to describe the work of the Holy Spirit (John 14:16 et al.). It is the comfort which, as Paul says elsewhere, we receive first of all from God 'who comforts us in our troubles, so that we can comfort those in any trouble with the comfort we ourselves have received from God' (2 Corinthians 1:4). Christian comfort, according to Paul, does not consist of arguing problems out of existence but of standing alongside those in trouble and sharing their troubles with them.

The distinctiveness of a Christian's position in grief can be demonstrated by comparing Paul's words with the following extract from a letter from a second century pagan lady called Irene:

> Irene to Taonnophris and Philo, good comfort. I am sorry and weep over the departed one as I wept for Didymas. And all things, whatsoever were fitting, I have done, and all mine, Epaphroditus and Thermuthion and Philion and Plantas. But nevertheless against such things one can do nothing. Therefore comfort one another.[18]

The similarity of the closing words of both passages is striking. For Irene, however, comfort can only be based on resignation and shared helplessness in the face of the hostile force of death. For Paul the possibility of comfort has a better basis in hope but is still necessary precisely because of the inevitability of grief. To those experiencing a complicated grief in the church at Thessalonica. Paul offers the comfort of hope in the resurrection. He does so to clear away their eschatological confusion and bring them a resource for coping. He does not use it to deny the validity of their grief. Interestingly, however, it is denial that many contemporary Christians, including biblical commentators, prefer to hear.

Chapter 3

GRIEF BEYOND THE BIBLE

In surveying these narratives of bereavement in the Old and New Testaments, it has become clear that grief is a biblical phenomenon. Important characters are shown to grieve when they lose by death significant persons in their lives. When this happens the depictions of grief are realistic and psychologically accurate. The symptoms described fit the circumstances of the losses in a way that is remarkable to anyone conversant with the contemporary study of the processes of bereavement. This is true over a wide range of authorship, dates and theological backgrounds.

Another striking feature of these stories is that the religious beliefs of the protagonists, if mentioned at all, seem to make no practical difference to their actual experience of grief. In the Old Testament, the covenant love of Yahweh is not brought to bear as a means of comfort to those grieving. In the New Testament, even the doctrines of resurrection and the eternal life of believers are not used to mitigate the pains of bereavement. Indeed, in a number of passages the full flow of grief is depicted alongside a strong expression of resurrection faith. In the single passage where 'hope' is used as a 'comfort' for grieving people, we have seen that the use of these words indicates that Paul is offering a resource for coping with the pain of grief by putting the death of Christians into a meaningful theological context. He does not use them as a means of denying the validity or the existence of grief.

The total picture leads us to the surprising, perhaps even shocking, conclusion that the Bible does not use religious faith or even belief in any form of life after death as a means of modifying the experience of those who lose loved ones through death. Biblical people — including Jesus himself — simply grieve!

The survey of commentaries on these texts has also unearthed another equally noteworthy feature — the resistance on the part of biblical commentators to the obvious. The vast majority seem to assume that the full pain of grief is incompatible with strong religious belief, especially when this involves faith in an afterlife. So Old Testament scholars reduce the varied depiction of human pain to textual considerations. New Testament commentators fall prey to an implicit docetism when faced with a grieving Jesus; or claim that a group of grieving people cannot be Christians; or insist that Paul's pastoral support of grieving people implies a prohibition on grief.

The reactions of these scholars are not something peculiar to them as a group. They seem to be reflecting a tendency found among many Christians. We have a difficulty with grief. Somewhere at the back of our minds is a suspicion that we should not suffer it; or if we do, that it should not feel so painful as it does or last so long; that perhaps to feel the full force of grief is incompatible with our faith; that by experiencing what is common to humanity we are denying what we claim to believe. Perhaps, for some of us, the refuge of what we assume to be our faith is a welcome relief. A 'celebration' is easier to cope with than a funeral. We turn with joy to a triumphant faith which buoys us up and mitigates our pain — but at the cost of suppression of part of our humanity, with dire consequences for our future physical, emotional and spiritual health.

Each reader must judge whether this is a fair description of the struggle many Christians have with grief. For me it simply reflects the experience of pastoral practice. What the first part of this book has shown is this: wherever such attitudes have come from they have not emerged from the Bible! The real origin of this strong element of denial in Christian grieving, the way it is embedded in our contemporary thinking and its consequences in our lives — this is the subject matter of the rest of this book. Before describing its origins, however, it is worth reflecting on how long this tendency has been present in Christian thinking. It is not merely a twentieth century phenomenon.

Aristeides

Aristeides was a Christian living in Athens during the second century AD. About a century before Aristeides emerges into the light of history, Paul had made his famous visit to Athens following his retreat from Thessalonica and Beroea as a result of Jewish-led opposition. He had made a memorable speech on the Areopagus where, as Luke tells us, 'All the Athenians and the foreigners who lived there spent their time doing nothing but talking about and listening to the latest ideas' (Acts 17:21). He was in the philosophical capital of the world and was breathing a different intellectual atmosphere from the synagogues where he usually preached, but the breadth of his cultural experience and learning was more than a match for the occasion.

Most of his hearers were of the Stoic or Epicurean schools of philosophy — thinkers who, although at variance among themselves, shared a distinctly sceptical view of life after death. They listened with interest to Paul until he mentioned the word 'resurrection', at which point the gathering broke up in embarrassment. Some sneered at the idea, others said, 'Some other time, perhaps!'

It was not that the Athenian philosophers had never come across the idea of life after death before. Important strands of Greek philosophy, most notably those originating in the teaching of Plato, had for a long time taught the immortality of the soul. If Paul had come preaching a form of Neoplatonism, both Stoics and Epicureans would quickly have rallied their arguments. A lively debate might have followed. It was the kind of controversy they delighted in. What caused them to snigger and slink away was the concept of resurrection, literally the 'standing up again' of dead people. It was too crude, too materialistic an idea for cultured Greeks. The distinction will become very important for us in the next part of this book.

But Paul had, against all odds, made a handful of converts, including a man called Dionysius, whose name would be adopted by a later generation to promote a mystical version of Christianity. Perhaps it was to the descendents of this little group of new Christians that Aristeides owed his faith.

So, a century or so after Paul's visit to Athens, a century also after Paul had sent his pastoral advice to the grieving Christians of Thessalonica, Aristeides, a Christian Athenian philosopher, sat down to write. Much had changed in the history of Christianity in those hundred years or so. The church was much larger; it had spread over a far greater geographical area; it encompassed a greater variety of peoples and cultures; it had come into contact with and had to confront a variety of ideas; it had had to battle against heresy in its own ranks; but most of all it had encountered fierce persecution. Not the minor synagogue-led riots that had characterized Paul's early missionary career — rather the sustained, powerful onslaught of the might of the Roman Empire.

Sometimes this had happened at the personal instigation of particular emperors such as Nero and Domitian. Sometimes it had affected particular areas and provinces at the whim of a governor or council. The Christian church had become an illegal, misrepresented and slandered sect. Thousands of Christians had been imprisoned, executed or suffered horrible deaths in the amphitheatres of the empire.

Many of the great minds of the church had concentrated on writing defences of the faith addressed to emperors or local authorities. These writers were the Apologists. There had been Justin and Quadratus; later there would be Tatian, Athenagoras, Theophilus, Tertullian. But at this moment it was Aristeides.

The *Apology* of Aristeides is a beautiful and moving piece of writing. His defence of Christian teaching and living, addressed probably to the Emperor Antoninus Pius presents Christians in a most attractive light. In particular he extols their quiet good works and the benefits of their life-style to the well-being of the empire. He does not hesitate to claim that 'on account of them there flows forth the beauty that is in the world' and that 'the world stands by reason of the intercession of Christians'.[1]

What is of interest here, however, is Aristeides' description of Christians in bereavement. Here is the passage in question:

> And if any righteous person of their number passes away from the world they rejoice and give thanks to God, and they follow his body, as if he were moving from one place to another: and when a child is born to any one of them, they praise God, and if again it chance to die in its infancy, they praise God mightily, as for one who has passed through the world without sins. And if again they see that one of their number has died in his iniquity or in his sins,

over this one they weep bitterly and sigh, as over one who is about to go to punishment: such is the ordinance of the law of the Christians, O king, and such is their conduct.[2]

It is obvious that we are here breathing a very different atmosphere from that of the Old and New Testaments. In only a hundred years, Christian thinking about bereavement — at least among the Greek Christians whom Aristeides knew — has undergone a paradigm shift. Nothing approaching what Aristeides writes here can be found in the Bible or the earlier sub-apostolic writings. Whether or not the majority of Christians really lived like this, it stands as testimony to what was clearly seen as an ideal of Christian conduct. Here is a list of some striking features of this passage:

(1) The response to the death of a fellow Christian is to be joy and thanksgiving. The expression of grief is implicitly excluded.
(2) A Christian funeral is not an occasion for the public expression of mourning but rather a time of celebration.
(3) Death is seen not as an end — with the hope of a new beginning in resurrection — but as a transition. The Christian has simply moved home.
(4) If the birth of a child is a cause for praise, the death of that child in infancy is even more so since the child has died without sin. One can only imagine the effect of conformity to this practice upon Christian parents.
(5) The expression of grief is only appropriate for someone who has died in sin and who is therefore seen as going to punishment. This is, unwittingly, a particularly cruel twist of the knife for Christians who cannot contain their feelings. What are tears saying about the supposed fate of the loved one?

Already therefore, somewhere around the year AD 150, we can discern two very different Christian attitudes to bereavement. One is based on the Bible and allows the full expression of grief, even when the doctrine of resurrection is clearly in view. The second, which must have an extra-biblical origin, suppresses the expression of grief as unworthy of a truly Christian life-style. The distinction is a contemporary as well as a second century one. Many Christians today would feel sympathy for all or some of Aristeides' ideals. A great many more would feel confusion and sense an incongruity between what they experience and what they have come to believe ought to be their response to the death of someone they love.

In order to understand where Aristeides' ideals originate, we must go back in time into another stream of human culture and experience.

PART II
Immortality and the Suppression of Grief

Chapter 4

PLATO: IMMORTALITY AS A CURE FOR GRIEF

We have discovered Christians in the mid-second century using the idea of life after death as a reason not to grieve. We have seen moreover that this is not a biblical idea, that in the Bible grief is treated as a natural and normal phenomenon with no hint that it should be suppressed. Nevertheless the suppression of grief has remained a strong tendency within Christianity and is very much with us today, even among Christians who take their Bibles seriously.

We are therefore faced with a number of questions. Where did the idea come from that grief is incompatible with belief in life after death? How did it enter the stream of Christian consciousness? Why has it become so influential in the lives of ordinary Christians — the kind of Christians who may be reading this book or their friends? These are the questions that this part of the book is concerned with. This chapter addresses the first two of these questions and the next chapter the third. The answers to the questions focus on two of the most hugely influential figures in the history of Western thought: Plato and Augustine.

Plato and Socrates

To begin the search we must stay in Aristeides' city of Athens, the centre of Greek culture and philosophy, but travel a further five centuries back in time. In around 388 BC the philosopher Plato returned to his native Athens to set up his famous school of philosophy known as the *Academy*. He had been away for eleven years, travelling mainly in Italy and Sicily, where he had been involved in teaching the children of the aristocracy (not always with great success!) and had picked up and was beginning to develop some very exciting ideas. According to his later pupil Aristotle he had learned from Pythagorean teachers the possibility that the human soul is immortal.[1]

But something else was smouldering in Plato's heart. He was still angry and bitter over the death in 399 BC of his beloved teacher and friend, Socrates. Socrates had been a powerful and influential teacher. He had gathered around him an eager and admiring group of intelligent young men from the upper classes of Athenian life, including Plato himself. They had been impressed by his penetrating questioning and his insistence on following the truth, as it was perceived, wherever it led.

The events leading to Socrates' death began with a political coup in Athens, led by a group known as 'the Thirty'. These men attempted to draw Socrates into their plans but, according to Plato, he refused and remained aloof from political involvement. Nevertheless, when 'the Thirty' fell from power, Socrates was associated with them in the minds of the reactionary forces now controlling Athens. He was put on trial accused of the twin crimes of 'impiety' and 'corrupting' the minds of the young[2] because of his questioning of traditional attitudes towards the gods. Plato wrote an account of Socrates' defence of himself while on trial for his life, known as the *Apology*. Although, at this point, Socrates is portrayed as being agnostic about what happens after death, Plato goes to great lengths to show us that his master and hero was not afraid to die. The death penalty was, however, inevitable and the manner of Socrates' dying will concern us shortly.

On setting up the Academy, Plato systematically set about defending Socrates' memory. He produced a prolific output of writings in the form of dialogues between Socrates and his pupils and opponents in which Socrates is, of course, the main speaker. Because Plato chose to write in this form, it is well-nigh impossible to unravel precisely which of the ideas being expressed were original to Socrates and which were Plato's. Certainly Plato does not hesitate to honour Socrates by putting on his lips some of the ideas which he himself was developing and for which he was to become famous, a method deemed perfectly normal in the ancient world, if confusing to the modern mind. Central to all that Plato wrote is his passion for Socrates' memory. As one scholar put it, Plato was 'bitterly hurt and angered by the judicial murder of Socrates' and in the dialogues he set out to 'paint a series of miniatures which would at once perpetuate the memory of his friend and reveal by what manner of men he had been put to death'.[3]

Plato was attempting to deal, over a decade after the event, with a death with which he had not yet come to terms. What is of interest for this study is that, during precisely the same period, he was developing his most characteristic ideas, those with which we would nowadays associate the word 'Platonic'. What were these ideas? They can be summarized as follows:

> Among the chief dialogues which may with some probability be assigned to the two decades following the foundation of the Academy are the *Meno*, *Phaedo*, *Symposium*, *Republic*, and *Phaedrus*. These works reveal for the first time the characteristically Platonic philosophy, whose twin pillars are the belief in a world of intelligible Forms or 'Ideas' existing independently of the things we see and touch and the belief in an immortal soul existing in separation from the body, both before birth and after death. It is the philosophy of a spirit which turns away from this mortal region to set its hopes on things beyond the reach of time and change.[4]

Central to this Platonic world-view is the concept of the natural immortality of the human soul. This idea appears first in the *Meno* where Plato is concerned not so much with life after death as with pre-existence. Socrates here uses the knowledge of an uneducated slave-boy to demonstrate that we all have stored information from a previous existence. To learn is to remember!

The idea of immortality has its clearest exposition, however, in that dialogue which takes place at the deathbed of Socrates, the *Phaedo*. This is more than coincidence and is so crucial to our investigation that it merits examination in some detail.

The Death of Socrates

Phaedo is depicted as one of the young men in Socrates' entourage. He had been present, with others, at the execution of the beloved master. One day he meets a group of friends who had not been present. One of them, Echecrates, presses him for an account of what happened. He tells them who else was at the deathbed, remarking pointedly that Plato was not there because he was ill. This is an interesting statement because it is the only occasion in any of the dialogues on which Plato mentions himself by name. Why should Plato choose to do so here? It is possible, of course, that it is a simple statement of fact. It is equally possible that Plato explains his absence so as to be able to recount his own vivid memories through the lips of a fictitious character called Phaedo. The likelihood of this hypothesis becomes clearer when, at the end of the book, we find real emotion being described in the first person, a very rare phenomenon in a Platonic dialogue.

So, the scene is set in Socrates' cell on the day of his execution. Death is to be by poisoning. This way the condemned criminal is responsible for his own death. There is no executioner. Socrates is lying on his bed with his friends and pupils gathered around him. What could the conversation be about on such an occasion? Well, in this case, it is a philosophical discussion and the main area of debate is the immortality of the soul. Socrates expounds a number of technical arguments to prove this doctrine which need not concern us here.

What is most relevant is the discussion about the relationship between philosophy, life and death. For Socrates, as recorded by Plato, philosophy itself implies a radical distinction between body and soul. Because it is a purely mental exercise, philosophy is the cultivator of the soul and therefore at war with the impulses of the body:

> the body fills us with loves and desires and fears and all sorts of fancies and a great deal of nonsense, with the result that we never get an opportunity to think at all about anything . . . We are in fact convinced that if we are ever to have pure knowledge of anything, we must get rid of the body and contemplate things by themselves with the soul by itself. It seems, to judge from the argument, that the wisdom which we desire and upon which we profess to have set our hearts will be attainable only when we are dead and not in our lifetime. (Phaedo, 111)

The body is therefore a nuisance. It gets in the way of true philosophy. The real person is the soul and this can act in freedom only when the body has been cast off in death. Death, for the philosopher, is something to be looked forward to, the time when we shall really be able to think! So Socrates can say:

> I want to explain to you how it seems to me natural that a man who has really devoted his life to philosophy should be cheerful in the face of death, and confident of finding the greatest blessing in the next world when his life is finished . . . If this is true and (philosophers) have actually been looking forward to death all their lives, it would of course be absurd to be troubled when the thing comes for which they have long been preparing and looking forward. (Phaedo, 107)

This sentiment is repeated at several points throughout the dialogue and might indeed be said to sum up its major thrust. Socrates then can logically make his famous but rather shocking assertion for those who today take up the study of philosophy that *true philosophers make dying their profession and that to them of all men death is least alarming.* (Phaedo, 113)

So, according to Plato, the true philosopher has no business being afraid of death. And the reason for this is that death is not really death at all. It is death only of the body which is merely something which gets in the way of the real contemplation of things. The soul, the real identity of the person, is, in any case, immortal. So why be afraid?

This assertion of course has its converse and this is of great importance if we are to see anything of what might be going on in Plato behind the confident words. On the one hand, philosophy, which asserts that the soul is immortal, is a defence against the fear of death. Similarly, evidence of the fear of death is a sure sign of a lack of real philosophy.

> So if you see any one distressed at the prospect of dying . . . it will be proof enough that he is a lover not of wisdom but of the body. As a matter of fact, I suppose he is also a lover of wealth and reputation; one or the other or both. (Phaedo, 113,114)

Any such fear must therefore be resisted firmly by the would-be philosopher.

Socrates, of course practises what he preaches. In the latter part of the book we see him as the perfect paradigm of the philosopher facing death. This is vividly portrayed in the last pages of the *Phaedo* as we come to the narration of the last moments of Socrates. As expected, Socrates approaches death with perfect composure and not a hint of distress. He is able to think about the most inconsequential of practical details: 'I prefer to have a bath before drinking the poison,' he says, 'rather than give the women the trouble of washing me when I am dead.' And so Socrates takes the poison and 'quite calmly and with no sign of distaste, he drained the cup in one breath'.

Socrates' peaceful end is then described for us. One classical scholar has compared Plato's account with what is known of hemlock poisoning from other ancient accounts as well as from modern toxicology to show that even the description of symptoms is distorted to emphasize the soul's release from the body.[5] Cold and numbness begin at Socrates' feet and gradually proceed up his body until death is complete: the soul has gone. Socrates' last words are significant: 'Crito, we ought to offer a cock to Asclepius. See to it and don't forget.' The offering to Asclepius was a thanksgiving for healing. The point is underlined: this is not really a death at all!

Plato and Grief

So much for Socrates, who has remained true to his philosophical principles to the end. But what of his companions, including, perhaps, Plato himself? How are they seen to be coping with the death of their hero? Here we have spelt out for us the Platonic attitude to grief in the light of the doctrine of the immortality of the soul.

This begins to become evident when one of the group called Crito asks a practical and apparently perfectly sensible question about burial and is subjected to a tirade from the master for not having taken in the implications of his teaching. One such implication is that grief is absolutely forbidden. Here is Socrates' response to the question.

> As far as my long and elaborate explanation that when I have drunk the poison I shall remain with you no longer, but depart to a state of heavenly happiness, this *attempt to console both you and myself* seems to be wasted on him. You must give one assurance to Crito for me . . . that when I am dead I shall not stay but depart and be gone. That will help Crito to bear it more easily, and to keep him from being distressed on my account when he

sees my body being burned or buried as if something dreadful were happening to me; or from saying at the funeral that it is Socrates whom he is laying out or carrying to the grave or burying. Believe me, my dear friend Crito, *mis-statements are not merely jarring in their immediate contexts; they also have a bad effect upon the soul*. No, you must keep *your spirits up* and say that it is only my body that you are burying; and you can bury it as you please, in whatever way you think is most proper. (Phaedo, 178,179)

I have italicized certain phrases in this speech. They could be seen, on one level, as chinks in the armour, of Socrates himself. It is important, however, to think of Plato, over twelve years later, thinking back on a scene which he either remembered or imagined and putting these words into the mouth of his friend. Could he be, in the very act of writing, using this teaching to 'console' both himself and others? Is it he that finds 'mis-statements' about death and immortality 'jarring' and creating a 'bad effect upon the soul'? Is Plato himself striving to 'keep his spirits up'?

What follows is almost unique in Platonic writing. As the book draws to its close, we encounter a fascinating fragment of psychological realism. Socrates' friends give vent to a perfectly natural outpouring of grief. Immediately Socrates himself turns upon them with a rigid defence against any show of emotion — including, incidentally one of literature's outstanding examples of sexist prejudice! The passage is worth quoting in full:

Up till this time most of us had been fairly successful in keeping back our tears; but when we saw that he was drinking, that he had actually drunk it, we could do so no longer; in spite of myself the tears came pouring out, so that I covered my face and wept broken-heartedly — not for him but for my own calamity in losing such a friend. Crito had given up even before me and had gone out when he could not restrain his tears. But Apollodorus, who had not stopped crying even before, now broke out into such a storm of passionate weeping that he made everyone in the room break down except Socrates himself, who said 'Really, my friends, what a way to behave! Why, that was my main reason for sending away the women, to prevent this sort of disturbance; because I am told that one should make one's end in a tranquil frame of mind. Calm yourselves and try to be brave.' (Phaedo, 182)

In these few words we have contrasted for us the natural expression of grief and its prohibition on the basis of the doctrine of the immortality of the soul. What may be of even greater significance is Phaedo's comment at this point:

> *This made us feel ashamed and we controlled our tears.*
> (Phaedo, 182)

A most important precedent is being set here. For the first time in Western literature we are informed that the expression of grief is something of which to be ashamed. In the interests of philosophy, tears are to be controlled. The encouragement of the stiff upper lip, which we tend to associate with the English public school, has its origin here in classical antiquity. It comes at the end of a strenuous exertion of the mind to prove that the human soul is immortal and in the context of one man's attempt to recount a death which haunted his life.

Plato takes up the theme of immortality again in the most famous of his writings, the *Republic*, his description of the ideal state.[6] In the last section, Book X, after yet more 'proofs' of the doctrine, seen by some as a supplement to the *Phaedo*, he gives us a vivid pictorial image of how the idea of immortality is to be understood: the Myth of Er.

Er was a warrior killed in battle who returned to life on his funeral pyre several days later. He recounts what he witnessed in the future life. This is described in picturesque detail but the essence of the story is that each soul after death undertakes a thousand year journey into heaven or under the earth during which it receives temporary (for all but the worst sinners) punishments or rewards depending upon its conduct in the past life. When this is finished the souls are taken to another place where they are given a vision of a mythological structure of the universe. Here, taking turns by lot, each soul chooses a sample life which is to be the form of its next earthly existence. The fate of each human being is thus chosen by each soul before birth. This is Plato's theodicy. 'God is blameless.'

Here is the Platonic vision of the relationship between soul and body. The soul is not merely the part of the person which survives the death and dissolution of the body. It is the real person who by a series of reincarnations takes up and discards any number of bodies with their accompanying earthly lives like so many garments. The body is an accidental and temporary condition chosen well or badly in a heavenly lottery.

In the *Republic* Plato also makes mention of grief and, as we may expect, it is seen in a negative light. In one passage, for example, Plato forbids grief to the 'Guardians', the elect militia of his Republic. To ensure their freedom from such weakening emotions the literature which forms part of their education is to be censored to remove all trace of it. Even Homer is not to be spared.

In another passage, this time in Book X itself, Plato deals with the problem of grief in literature. His target here is tragic drama. Why, he asks, should we applaud poets who encourage us to feel, by empathy with the characters, emotions — such as grief — which we ought to be ashamed of in real life? Indeed the very experience of sympathy itself is fraught with emotional danger. In Plato's ideal Republic, the well-schooled individual, protected by a philosophy teaching the immortality of the soul, will have no place for grief.

A Platonic Theory of Grief

The influence of Plato on the thinking of the Western world has been immeasurable. It is well acknowledged that at the heart of that influence there lies his doctrine of the immortality of the soul — a soul which not only lives on after the body but which existed eternally before it. What has not always been recognized is that this idea has been accompanied by the practical ideal of the suppression of grief. It is not simply that we happen to see grief suppressed in practice in those same texts which teach immortality, but that the two features belong to the same logical process. In Plato theory and practice are consistent. It is possible to set out a Platonic theory of grief which would look something like the following.

(1) The human soul is immortal. When the body dies the soul continues to live. Death does not interrupt the life of the soul and is merely a transition.
(2) The soul not only outlives the body which it currently inhabits, but existed before it. Its present body is a random choice, having little to do with the nature of the soul. Real personhood resides in the soul.

(3) The body is a hindrance to the soul's fulfilment of its potential. Its loss in death is no loss at all but, rather, an advantage. There is nothing to be grieved for.
(4) Grief is not only illogical but a weakness. It is part of the frailty of that very body which is to be despised.
(5) The well-educated individual therefore has no place for grief. He should suppress it in himself and avoid such things as literature or drama which may stimulate it.

There may be those who would be grateful that Plato has sublimated his own grief over the death of Socrates by writing the Socratic dialogues. Nevertheless, he has left us, I believe, a dubious legacy regarding grief. In any case, we are a long way, in thought and spirit, from the writings of the biblical authors we have considered.

Plato and the Early Church Fathers

Why should the thinking, writing and experience of a pagan philosopher living four hundred years before the birth of Christ be so important in a study of Christian attitudes to grieving? I believe that we shall see the answer to that question most fully when, in the next chapter, we look into the life and teaching of Augustine. First, however, it is important to look briefly at a tendency developing gradually in the Christian mind in the first four hundred years or so of the church's life.

As the church moved westwards from Palestine, it entered more and more deeply into a world dominated by Greek ideas. Christianity had been born in the Judaic thought patterns of the Old Testament and later Jewish writings. More and more, however, Christians were compelled to give expression to their beliefs in terms of the vocabulary and categories of Greek philosophy. Among the philosophies to choose from in the classical world Platonism, although already centuries old, was enjoying a revival and sense of ascendancy during this period. The great Neoplatonic writers, Plotinus (AD 205–270) and his pupil, Porphyry of Tyre (c.250–c.305) AD, a fierce opponent of Christianity, flourished in the mid to late third century, but they were part of a trend beginning long before them and their ideas persisted much later.

Writers like these repeated Plato's views about the immortality of the human soul but expressed them in even stronger language. The body was frequently referred to as a 'tomb' or a 'prison' from which the soul, the real person, was released at death. Such ideas were also encapsulated in the teaching of the Gnostic heresies against which orthodox Christians battled in the early centuries. Central to the teaching of most of the diverse sects known by the collective term of Gnostics was the idea of the soul as a divine spark which had to be liberated from evil matter by a series of initiations into secret knowledge or *gnosis*.

Very early Christian writers such as Tatian (c.120–post-174) and Irenaeus (c.130–c.200) opposed such ideas, but the pressure to adapt Christian thinking to a new intellectual environment became more and more difficult to resist. The trend towards hellenisation (the adoption of Greek ideas) is usually associated with the Christian school of Alexandria, represented by such great writers as Clement (died c.214) and Origen (185–254) who believed the soul to be not only immortal but to exist before birth. The process however was very common during the time of the church fathers.

For one thing, when fighting a battle of ideas, it is sometimes necessary to advance into your opponent's territory. This sometimes means attempting to demonstrate his errors in his own terms. This happened particularly in the struggle against Gnosticism. But often, as a larger battle was being won, a more subtle defeat was taking place as the enemy's thought processes were being assumed. So a slightly embarrassed Origen defends his use of Platonic language in opposing the teaching of the first philosophical opponent of Christianity, a man called Celsus.

> Do not suppose that it is not consistent with Christian doctrine when in my reply to Celsus I accepted the opinions of those philosophers who have affirmed the immortality or the survival of the soul.[7]

The fact was that much biblical language appeared naively vague when seen in the light of analytic philosophical thinking. The Greek word *psyche*, for example, had been used in the New Testament to express the idea of *life*, *self* or *personhood* without any clear definition. Platonic philosophy offered to give such a term a clearly defined content. It became easy to read back into the Scriptures or other Jewish and early Christian writings a meaning which would never have occurred to those who wrote them. 'Soul' came to mean in many minds a substantial entity, quite separate from the body, immortal if not also pre-existent, which would be released to freedom at the death of the body.[8]

Death itself thus also began to change its meaning. It became less what Paul called 'the last enemy' and more a longed for liberation into an immaterial state of blessedness. Grief, which had co-existed with the biblical doctrine of death and resurrection, was becoming less and less consistent with perceived Christian teaching. The *Apology* of Aristeides which we have looked at comes very early in this process. Nevertheless, it is easy to perceive the stream in which it stands. More importantly, the stage is being set for the dramatic entrance of Augustine.

Chapter 5

AUGUSTINE: THE TRIUMPH OF IMMORTALITY OVER GRIEF

In the year AD 385 or thereabouts, Augustine, the young Professor of Rhetoric in Milan, sat with his friend Alypius in the garden of the house in which they were both lodging. His mind was in turmoil and his agitated state could be seen from his movements. His hands would tug at his hair or beat his forehead. From time to time he would hug his knees to his body. He was in torment, and as he recalled the incident many years later,[1] he wondered how a single mind could be so divided against itself. He was wrestling with the decision as to whether to give up his old way of life and commit himself to the only kind of Christianity which now seemed valid to him: a life of celibacy.

The crisis had been sparked off by a conversation which had just taken place in the house. The pair had been visited by a fellow countryman from the Roman province of Africa on a matter of business. The visitor had noticed a copy of Paul's epistles on a table and, identifying himself as a Christian, began to speak of the ascetic life of the desert father Antony and told of the recent conversion of two friends of his to a life of celibacy on reading Antony's story. When the visitor left, Augustine rushed out into the garden, followed by his friend, concerned for his welfare.

Stepping-stones

A number of aspects of Augustine's life had contributed to this moment. As a youth he had rejected the Christian faith of his mother, Monica. There were two main reasons for this. Firstly he was unwilling to accept the moral discipline which Christianity would impose on him. Looking back on this later, he saw it as a victory of the world of the senses over the immaterial world: 'I turned my pulsating mind away from the spiritual towards the material.' There were also intellectual considerations. Christianity seemed a crude and unsophisticated faith to the bright, young Augustine finding his place among the intellectual elite of the thriving Roman province of Africa.

Since he had been in Milan, however, things had begun to change. He had brought his mother to stay with him and her influence on him at this point is very marked. She had persuaded him to put away the concubine with whom he had lived for thirteen years in order to contract a more socially advantageous marriage. While waiting for his bride-to-be, however, he had found even temporary celibacy impossible and taken a mistress. The whole area of sexuality was beginning to bother him.

His religious ideas were also in transition. For a time he had dabbled with Manichaeism, an ascetic teaching originating in Persia which saw good and evil as equal forces locked in eternal conflict. But now he was warming towards Christianity. This had a lot to do with the presence of his mother, but he had also come under the influence of Ambrose, the saintly bishop of Milan, whose teaching Augustine had been surprised to find intelligent and relevant to his own intellectual and spiritual struggles. Ambrose was a Christian preacher with pronounced Platonic leanings.[2]

It was at this point that he was given some 'Platonic books', recently translated into his native Latin by Victorinus. It is unlikely that these were works by Plato himself. More probably they were writings of more recent Neoplatonists like Plotinus or Porphyry. Their effect on him was dynamic. Their strong dualism between body and soul chimed with his own sense of discomfort with his sexuality. On an intellectual level they provided him with the kind of spiritual way of envisaging God that he had been seeking.

Augustine saw his adoption of Platonic philosophical ideas as an important stepping stone towards his acceptance of Christianity. So important were these books to him that, as we see him reflecting upon them later in life, it is clear that, despite his own protests, they rivalled the Bible in their impact upon him.

> I believe that it was by your will that I came across these books before I studied Scripture . . . For if I had not come across these books until after I had been formed in the mould of your Holy Scriptures and had learned to love you through familiarity with them, the Platonist teaching might have swept me from my foothold on the solid ground of piety, and even if I had held firm to the spirit in which the Scriptures had imbued me for my salvation, I might have thought it possible for a man who read nothing but the Platonist books to derive the same spirit from them alone. (Confessions, 154,155)

One of Augustine's biographers sums up his state of mind at this point.

> Neoplatonic spirituality and the stress on interiority and on liberation from the distractions of the external world, sharpened Augustine's feeling of being pulled in two directions with his sexual drive as a downward pull.[3]

This is the background to Augustine's state of mind as he sat in that garden. What happened next was not only life-transforming for Augustine but an epochal event in the history of Christianity. It has been compared in its impact to the conversion of Saul on the Damascus Road.

Augustine was struggling with the decision of whether or not to become a Christian. Because of his personal circumstances and the influence of the books he had recently read, he conceived his dilemma as a struggle between body and soul. Even more specifically, it could be described as a battle between sexuality and celibacy, which he now saw as the ideal of the Christian life. In his dilemma he pictured the 'chaste beauty of Continence' beckoning him to cross the barrier of his indecision. The words he heard her whisper to him are significant:

> Close your ears to the unclean whispers of your body, so that it may be mortified. It tells you of things that delight you but not such things as the law of the Lord your God has to tell. (Confessions, 176)

Augustine, feeling himself about to lose control, stood up and left Alypius. Going to a more private part of the garden, he threw himself onto the ground beneath a fig tree and burst into tears. His weeping was interrupted by the sound of a child's voice singing in a neighbouring house. Under such circumstances the

words were taken as divine direction: *Tolle, lege*, 'Pick up and
read'. He went back to where he had been sitting with his friend
and picked up the copy of Paul's letters which was lying there.
Opening it at random his eyes fell on part of Romans 13:13,14
which can be translated in the following way from the Latin
version which Augustine was reading: 'Not in revelling and
drunkenness, not in lust and wantonness, not in quarrels and
rivalries. Rather, arm yourselves with the Lord Jesus Christ;
spend no more thought on nature and nature's appetites.'

For Augustine, this settled the matter. His indecision van-
ished. All that remained was to tell his friend Alypius and then
to go in and inform his mother who, needless to say, was
overjoyed. Augustine does not inform us of the reactions of
either his mistress or his fiancée! Rather, he sums up his
experience thus: 'You converted me to yourself, so that I no
longer desired a wife.' Augustine had decided to become a
Christian; at the same time he had determined to become
celibate. From this moment on he was to be committed to a
Christianity undergirded by Platonism.

The Beatific Vision

If the Platonic flavour of Augustine's Christianity affected his
view of sexuality and marriage, it just as surely, had an impact
on his view of life after death.

Shortly after his conversion, Augustine and Monica were on a
journey from Milan to their native Africa. During a stop in the
town of Ostia, they were leaning together out of a window
'wondering what the eternal life of the saints would be like'. This
shared contemplation, we are told, resulted for them both in a
sort of *out-of-body experience* which Augustine described in
these words:

> Our conversation led us to the conclusion that no bodily pleasure
> however great it might be and whatever earthly light might shed
> lustre upon it, was worthy of comparison, or even of mention
> beside the happiness of the life of the saints . . . And while we
> spoke of the eternal Wisdom, longing for it and straining for it
> with all the strength of our hearts, for one fleeting instant we
> reached out and touched it. Then, with a sigh, leaving our spiritual
> harvest bound to it, we returned to the sound of our own speech

in which each word has a beginning and an ending . . . (Confessions, 197)

There follows a long description of what, on the basis of this experience, Augustine was for long afterwards to consider the state of the blessed to be like. One short excerpt sums this up:

> Suppose that this state were to continue and all other visions of things inferior were to be removed, so that the single vision entranced and absorbed the one who beheld it and enveloped him in inward joys in such a way that for him life was eternally the same as that instant of understanding for which we had longed so much — would not this be what we are to understand by the words 'Come and share the joy of your Lord?' (Confessions, 198)

It will be evident that a particular view of heaven emerges from the description of this experience. It is immaterial, purely spiritual and static. Although, in later writings Augustine was to, rather grudgingly, allow for the presence of some kind of bodies in heaven, the disembodied 'beatific vision' was his most characteristic contribution to the Christian idea of life after death.[4] It has been summed up in this way:

> The heaven of which Augustine had a foretaste in the garden of Ostia was the hereafter of platonizing Greek philosophy . . . It was then that he decided that a mental, spiritual union with God meant the ultimate happiness — a decision of momentous consequence for Christian history.[5]

But why should one man's spiritual experience be so monumentally important for the history of Christianity? Probably, after the New Testament writers, no Christian thinker has exerted such a huge influence as Augustine, Bishop of Hippo, as he later became. His writings, particularly his *Confessions*, a remarkable spiritual autobiography in which he examines the inner workings of his mind in the form of an extended prayer, and his theological magnum opus, the *City of God*, have shaped the way in which Christians, especially in the West, have thought for fourteen centuries.

When Western Christianity split into two and subsequently fragmented further at the time of the Reformation, Augustine was the only one of the Church Fathers to hold equally powerful sway on both sides of the divide. His catholicity and asceticism appealed to the Roman Church while his views on predestination and divine grace influenced both Luther and Calvin and became axiomatic within Protestantism. Indeed, his influence can be said to go further. According to one writer:

> He was the most acute of Christian Platonists and did much to lay the foundations for the synthesis between Christianity and classical theism . . . Anselm, Aquinas, Petrarch (never without a pocket copy of the *Confessions*), Luther, Bellarmine, Pascal and Kierkegaard all stand in the shade of his broad oak. His writings were among the favourite books of Wittgenstein. He was the 'bête noir' of Nietzsche. His psychological analysis anticipated Freud.[6]

If this is true then Augustine's influence can be traced in mediaeval scholasticism, Western mysticism, the Reformation and Counter-Reformation, the Enlightenment, the Romantic movement, Existentialism, Psychoanalysis and modern philosophy! He has left the footprints of his thought on the minds of countless people who may never have read a word he wrote. Included in this stupendous legacy is the Platonic idea of the immortal soul, naturally surviving the body at death and contemplating the vision of God in immaterial blessedness. It is a concept quite distinct from the biblical view of resurrection and having, as we shall see, quite different practical consequences. As another writer puts it:

> Augustine began his career as a Christian priest and author with an idea of immortality of the soul which excludes resurrection of the body.[7]

Augustine and Grief

But this is a book about bereavement and grief. We have seen that Plato's exposition of the idea of immortality is presented in contexts where the expression of grief is explicitly condemned and suppressed. Is there any way of knowing the effect of Augustine's beliefs on the experience of grief? Fortunately there is; and we owe it, it has to be said, to Augustine's own honesty and acute psychological observation of his own emotions.

The *Confessions* contain two moving accounts of bereavement in the life of Augustine and, happily for us, one occurs in his pagan days and one very soon after his conversion. We thus have a unique opportunity to see the effect of his Platonised Christianity upon his experience of grief.

Grief for a friend

Early in his adult life, while still living in Africa, Augustine suffered the loss of a close yet unnamed friend through death. His description of his emotions is striking for the realism with which the various aspects of grief are depicted: the pain of the familiar, the sense of searching, the hopelessness, longing, unreality and even desire for death. It could all have come from a modern handbook on bereavement. The following is a short excerpt:

> All that we had done together was now a grim ordeal without him. My eyes searched everywhere for him, but he was not to be seen. I hated all the places we had known together, because he was not in them and they could no longer whisper to me, 'Here he comes!' as they would have done had he been alive but absent for a while . . . Tears alone were sweet to me, for in my heart's desire they had taken the place of my friend . . . I had no hope that he would come to life again nor was this what I begged for through my tears: I simply grieved and wept for I was heartbroken and had lost my joy . . . for I was sick and tired of living and yet afraid to die . . . I wondered that other men should live while he was dead for I had loved him as though he would never die. Still more I wondered that he should die and I remain alive, for I was his second self. (Confessions, 76,77)

Given a very close relationship, such an experience of grief now appears completely normal. To a modern bereavement counsellor much of what Augustine describes would be predictable, as would the fact that when grief is thus honestly admitted and felt, relief could be expected to come with time. So it was for Augustine:

> Little by little (time) pieced me together again by means of the old pleasures which I had once enjoyed. My sorrow gave way to them. (Confessions, 79)

One might say that, from a contemporary understanding of the grieving process, this grief of Augustine's was successful and satisfactory. It is described with the same honesty, if with more detail, as we have discovered in a number of biblical accounts.

However, the older Augustine, writing from the vantage point of his subsequent Platonic-Christian persona, does not see it at all in that way. In fact, he finds the grief which he experienced reprehensible: 'What madness to love a man as something more than human! What folly to grumble at the lot man has to bear!' He then goes on to tell us what *ought* to have happened:

> I knew, Lord, that I ought to offer it up to you for you would heal it. But this I would not do, nor could I, especially as I did not think of you as anything real and substantial. (Confessions, 78)

The normal symptoms of grief are in hindsight seen as stemming from a faulty view of God and an inability to appeal to him in the right way. Indeed as might be predicted the whole experience of grief is now seen as the result of a too close attachment to the things of the body and the senses and an inability to grasp spiritual and eternal realities.

For the Christian Augustine, the fullness of the enjoyment of God is related to freedom from the restrictions of the body and the material world. God himself, therefore, is a refuge from the pain of living in the body — and this includes the pain of bereavement. Even the Christian doctrines of incarnation and atonement, which might be seen as affirming the body, are used by Augustine to deny the validity of grief: 'Our Life himself came down into this world and took away our death.'

Grief for His Mother

Following the famous experience at the window in Ostia, Augustine's mother, Monica, it seems, began to lose interest in bodily life. Very soon afterwards, while still at Ostia, she died. Now, if a normal grief, viewed in hindsight, created problems for Augustine, we may imagine how complex would be the experience of losing, so soon after his conversion, a person as important and influential in his life as the indomitable Monica. The conflict between the natural reactions of grief and the repressive influence of a doctrine of immortality which has no place for such emotions, lies very close to the surface throughout Augustine's narrative. One writer comments significantly: 'As a philosopher he feels bound not to flinch'.[8] Again it might be most helpful simply to use Augustine's own words:

I closed her eyes and a great wave of sorrow surged into my heart. It would have overflowed into tears if I had not made a strong effort of will and stemmed the flow, so that the tears dried in my eyes. What a terrible struggle it was to hold them back! As she breathed her last the boy Adeodatus began to wail and only ceased his cries when we all checked him. I too felt that I wanted to cry like a child, but a more mature voice within me, the voice of my heart, bade me keep my sobs in check, and I remained silent. For we did not think it right to mark my mother's death with weeping and moaning, because such lamentations are the usual accompaniment of death when it is thought of as a state of misery or as total extinction. But she had not died in misery nor had she wholly died. Of this we were certain, both because we knew what a holy life she had led and also because our faith was real and we had sure reasons not to doubt it . . . You know, O Lord, how I suffered but my friends did not, and as they listened intently to my words, they thought that I had no sense of grief. But in your ears, where none of them could hear, I blamed myself for my tender feelings. I fought against the wave of sorrow and for a while it receded but then it swept upon me again with full force. It did not bring me to tears and no sign of it showed on my face, but I knew well enough what I was stifling in my heart. It was misery to feel myself so weak a victim of these human emotions, although we cannot escape them since they are the natural lot of mankind, and so I had the added sorrow of being grieved by my own feelings, so that I was tormented by a twofold agony. (Confessions, 200,201)

As we watch Augustine, his son and their friends around the deathbed of Monica we find ourselves in the presence of the same emotional process as occurred in the cell of Socrates. One can only feel sympathy for the poor young Adeodatus being sharply reprimanded for his tears at the death of his grandmother. For Augustine it is more complex. We see him locked in a complication of grief created by his vision of life after death. He is grieving for the loss of his mother, but his recently found faith tells him that she has not really died. Over and above his natural grief therefore he blames himself for the inconsistency of his feelings. Indeed another layer of complication occurs when he asks God to remove the pain and God apparently refuses. Thus, on the day of the funeral he finds himself trying to rationalize this lack of response from God. With the characteristic Christian urge to find a reason for everything, he says:

> I believe that this was because you wished to impress upon my memory, if only by this one lesson, how firmly the mind is gripped in the bonds of habit, even when it is nourished on the word of truth. (Confessions, 201)

Finally however 'alone in bed' he gave way to his tears:

> The tears which I had been holding back streamed down and I let them flow as freely as they would, making of them a pillow for my heart. On them it rested, for my weeping sounded in your ears alone, not in the ears of men who might have misconstrued it and despised it. (Confessions, 202)

Although they were a comfort at the time however the memory of those tears seems to rekindle a kind of guilt which has to be immediately defended against.

> And if (anyone) finds that I sinned by weeping for my mother, even if only for a fraction of an hour, let him not mock at me. . . Let him weep for my sins to you, the Father of all the brothers of your Christ. (Confessions, 203)

And his final verdict upon himself at this point is the rather rueful comment that 'perhaps I was guilty of too much worldly affection.' (Confessions, 203)

Summary

In these last two chapters, we have seen how, in the writings of the Western world's two leading proponents of the immortality of the soul, theory and practice go hand in hand. An immortalist philosophy leads to the logical conclusion that death is not real and leaves us with nothing to grieve for. Plato and Augustine are both consistent in maintaining that grief is illogical for someone holding such a view. We have seen in both cases, however, that natural emotions do not always comply with theory. Both these men experienced real and poignant grief: Plato for his teacher Socrates; Augustine for his mother Monica. It was the logic of both their positions, however, that if emotion conflicted with theory, it was emotion that was at fault and must be suppressed.

Thus we have observed both these intellectual giants making strenuous efforts to suppress the expression of natural grief at the death of their loved ones. We might say that, because of this, the griefs of both were never really dealt with. Perhaps Plato never came to terms with the death of Socrates or Augustine with the death of his mother (or, for that matter, the death of his son, Adeodatus, who died at the age of sixteen and receives a summary obituary in the *Confessions*). To what extent might such repressed grief have affected the thinking of such men? It is tempting to speculate on how the history of Christianity and of Western thought in general might have been different if these two men had dealt differently with their grief!

We can now discern two quite distinct attitudes to grief which have entered the Christian consciousness. One we might call the biblical approach. It is typified by characters in both Old and New Testaments who grieved openly — Abraham, Jacob, David, Jesus and the early Christians. We have seen that the hope of resurrection from the dead, which the New Testament characters at least held strongly, offered a resource for coping with grief but made no claims to eradicate it or declare it invalid.

The second approach we can now refer to as the Platonic–Augustinian view. If Plato was the first to give this attitude literary and philosophical expression, it was Augustine who 'baptized' it as semi-official Christian doctrine and ensured its dissemination down the centuries among countless Christians. It is based on the doctrine of the natural immortality of the soul and declares grief to be an inconsistent emotion which must be minimized if not suppressed altogether. Christians holding such a view will believe their grief to be a weakness and an evidence of lack of faith. If they are unable to repress it totally they will, like Plato and Augustine, feel ashamed of it.

Both these attitudes are with us among Christians today. Some may hold a consistent resurrectionist view and have no difficulty with admitting the need to grieve. Others may be consistent immortalists and deny grief its validity. Others, the majority perhaps, may hold either view inconsistently or vacillate between the two. No wonder we are confused!

It may still not be clear, however, why two different ways of conceiving life after death should have such different practical consequences. They may still look like two ways of saying what is essentially the same thing. There are implications of both of these views that we have not yet considered and to this we must turn our attention in the next part of the book.

PART III
Immortality or Resurrection?

Chapter 6

THE GROWTH OF RESURRECTION FAITH

It became clear in the first part of this book that a belief in resurrection is compatible with the experience and expression of grief. The New Testament writers had no hesitation in depicting both Jesus and the early Christians as grieving unashamedly when their loved ones died. What may not be clear at this point is *why* this should be so. Why should the biblical doctrine of resurrection not become, like the Platonic idea of the immortality of the soul, grounds for the denial or suppression of the common human need to grieve? What are the real distinctions between the two ideas which, after all, appear only to be two different ways of expressing the belief that there is life beyond death?

To begin to answer these questions, we shall, in this chapter, trace the development of the idea of resurrection through the biblical writings to discover something of its real nature. Before that, however, it may help to look at a particular way of classifying views of life after death.

Orientations to Death

The American anthropologist Frank Borkenam isolated three distinctive orientations towards death. He called them: (a) death-accepting, (b) death-denying, and (c) death-transcending.[1] He saw them as the dominant views of whole societies or civilisations and believed that fluctuations between them were important factors in the shaping of history. For Borkenam, a death-transcending orientation arises as a synthesis of the other two. He defines it as a belief which 'accepts death but aims at transcending it.' For this reason, although it is an ideal state towards which societies aspire, it can also be seen as somewhat unstable, being vulnerable to either of its constituent elements, acceptance or denial.

Borkenam sees Christianity, with its teaching on resurrection, as possibly the most stable and long-lasting of all historical attempts at death-transcendence. However, all through its history, it has been under threat from both death-accepting and death-denying ideas: views, that is, which claim, in one way or another, either that death is final or that death is not real. This has never been more true than at the present. In contemporary Western culture, it would be difficult to say which orientation is most dominant.

It is not necessary to follow Borkenam's theories in all their details to appreciate the helpfulness of his categories. I would like here to slightly redefine Borkenam's terms, thinking of them not as the monolithic views of entire civilisations but as attitudes which have always existed and which are to be found side by side in our contemporary pluralistic society:

A *death-denying* attitude is one in which the reality of death is ignored or repressed, in particular in relation to one's own death or that of one's loved ones. Life is lived in the pretence that death does not exist as a personal reality. This attitude may be conscious or unconscious.

A *death-accepting* attitude is one in which the existence of death is faced as a final, personal reality. It implies a belief in the end of personal existence at death. This may be held with great equanimity, with resignation, with protest or even with despair.

A *death-transcending* attitude is one in which the reality of death is accepted and perhaps even feared, but which embraces a belief in life after death with sufficient integrity to enable someone to look at death with hope and yet without denial.

It might be helpful to consider these three orientations from the perspective of personal bereavement. When faced with the death of someone they love, someone with a death-accepting orientation is, of course, likely to grieve deeply. For such a person a loss through death is final. There is nothing to be done to remedy it; there is simply pain to be endured. Although such a situation is indeed bleak, the person suffering it, will, at least, be facing the loss honestly. As we shall see later, this will be an advantage in terms of the grief process. However, there is a price to pay for this advantage. Honest grief comes at the cost of utter hopelessness. We might think of the letter of 'Irene' or the preconversion experience of Augustine as examples of this position.

For someone who has a death-denying attitude grief is likely to be much more problematic. If the reality of death is denied then so, in all likelihood, will be the reality of loss which death causes. This makes grief difficult to face. Its very existence is an enigma or an evidence of weakness. But if grief is not dealt with, it does not disappear. It is merely suppressed, creating immense psychological problems. I have argued that the 'Platonic-Augustinian' attitude to grief, based as it is on a belief in the immortality of the soul which denies that death affects the real person, is such a view. It encourages those who hold it to deny the force of their grief and to suppress its effects. Plato and his friends, the Christian community of Aristeides and the Platonic-Christian Augustine all show this attitude.

A death-transcending orientation, on the other hand, must surely be the most favourable to a satisfactory outcome from bereavement. Because such an attitude does not deny the reality of death, it will allow the full force of grief and offer the bereaved a realistic opportunity to work through the grieving process. At the same time, it will not leave them desolate but will provide a framework of hope as a resource to support them through the process.

If the Christian doctrine of resurrection is really a death-transcending idea then we begin to see why those who hold it in the New Testament are still able to deal honestly with their grief. As we trace its development in the rest of this chapter, therefore, the question to be answered is whether it meets the criteria for a truly death-transcending orientation. To qualify for this it must demonstrate the twin but paradoxical elements of an acceptance of the reality of death and the possibility of a hope beyond it.

The Fear of Sheol

The Old Testament does not tell us much about resurrection, but it is here that our search begins. When an Old Testament Israelite thought about what was to happen after death, he was most likely to do so in terms of Sheol. This seems sometimes to refer literally to 'the grave' but also to have been seen as a place of vague and shadowy existence which was not looked forward to with great relish if some of the psalms are anything to go by (read, for example Psalm 88!). In fact existence in Sheol could hardly be considered life at all. Most strikingly, it is often represented as a place where God is not. In their appeals to Yahweh, at least, the dread of Sheol for the Psalmists is the fear of being cut off from the community of those who praise 'the God of the living'.

In Isaiah 14 the prophet taunts the king of Babylon with the prospect of his descent to Sheol. Here he will be greeted by the shades of other great rulers who will still, apparently, be sitting on their thrones but have become 'weak'. At the same time, the literal 'grave' is still clearly in view including the maggots and worms. It must be noted that this is not a 'hell' to be contrasted with a 'heaven' to which good Israelites go. This shadow of the person in Sheol has been variously described as a sort of soul subsisting only so long as something of the body remains[2] or as 'the person reduced to its weakest possible state . . . an image of the body'.[3] It is this state that the pious psalmists pray to be delivered from by being kept alive (see Psalm 6 and many others). It soon becomes clear that language about Sheol and its inhabitants is not about life after death at all but a pictorial way of talking about death itself.

Such seems to be the majority view in the Old Testament. In terms of the categories outlined, it can be described as a 'death-accepting' orientation. Such a view however was not to remain unchallenged. In just a handful of psalms, the writers dare posit a hope that Sheol will not be the last word for the one who is in a personal relationship with Yahweh. The writer of Psalm 49, for example admits that

> the ransom for a life is costly, no payment is ever enough — that he should live on for ever and not see decay.

but, paradoxically, expresses the hope that

> God will redeem my life from Sheol; he will surely take me to himself.

It is Psalm 16, however, which caught the imagination of the early Christians because of the way it seemed to forecast the resurrection of Christ:

because you will not abandon me to Sheol, you will not let your
holy one see decay.

It is arguable, of course, that these psalmists were not expecting
resurrection at all but rather expressing the hope that, rather like
Enoch and Elijah, they would not die but be received straight into
the presence of God. In any case, however, we can certainly
make the following assertions about their expectations:

1. Sheol is a fate to be feared and is seen as the common lot of
humanity.
2. Escape from Sheol can only be envisaged as an exceptional
intervention of Yahweh.
3. Such an intervention is to be looked for only on the basis of
a relationship between Yahweh and the person concerned.

Yet in My Flesh shall I See God

The Wisdom literature of the Old Testament, particularly the
books of Job and Ecclesiastes, also expressed a dissatisfaction
with the orthodox Sheol-belief. It has been described as a kind
of existential protest literature[4] which, like the existentialist
writers of the twentieth century, accepted the reality of death
while protesting against it.

It is in this context that we read those striking words in the
Book of Job, when, from the heart of his undeserved suffering,
Job cries out:

> I know that my Redeemer lives, and that in the end he will stand
> upon the earth. And after my skin has been destroyed, yet in my
> flesh I will see God; I myself will see him with my own eyes — I
> and not another. How my heart yearns within me. (Job 19:25–27)

The textual reading of this passage is notoriously difficult. However, such an understanding as the NIV gives above can be
justified not simply as a prophetic foresight of New Testament
revelation but as a cry from the depths of someone whose
personal faith in God is being stretched to the limit.[5] The problem
with which the writer of Job struggles is that of theodicy — the
righteousness of God in view of the unjust suffering in the world.
How can God be seen as faithful to his promises if death marks the
boundary of his involvement with individual human beings?

It is this problem that contemporary scholars would see as the catalyst for the gradual emergence of a more transcendent view of life after death in the Old Testament.[5] In earlier writings, Israel's hope in Yahweh was expressed in terms of the prosperity of the nation. During and following the Exile this view was more difficult to maintain. It was possible to justify national suffering in terms of punishment for national sin. But what of the share of suffering endured by those who remained faithful to Yahweh? This more individualistic approach to rewards and punishments can already be seen in the writings of the exilic prophets Jeremiah and Ezekiel. If God is to be seen as faithful to those who put their trust in him, then this life cannot be seen as his only theatre of operation.

This context gives a particular shape to the Old Testament hope for life after death, such as it is. It is tied closely to the idea of God's faithfulness and to the integrity of the human person to whom God has pledged that faithfulness. There is no question of a natural condition of immortality beyond the shadowy state of Sheol which, as we have seen, is really death itself. Hope for life does not reside here but precisely in deliverance from Sheol. Without the activity of God such a deliverance would appear ludicrous; with the activity of the living God, anything but the bringing to life again of the whole person would be unthinkable.

This is already evident in Isaiah 26. It is possible that the prospect of resurrection here is a metaphorical reference to the return from exile. However, the language is significant. Of those who oppressed Israel, it is said:

> They are now dead, they live no more; those departed spirits (the 'shades' of Sheol) do not rise.

Of God's people, however, it is said:

> But your dead will live; their bodies will rise. You who dwell in the dust, wake up and shout for joy. Your dew is like the dew of the morning. The earth will give birth to her dead.

Life beyond death is pictured, not as a natural survival of part of the person, but as a resurrection of the whole — including the body. When there finally occurs, in the Book of Daniel, the one Old Testament verse which indisputably speaks of the life beyond death of individual human beings, the terms used are unequivocally those of resurrection: 'Multitudes who sleep in the dust of the earth will awake'(Daniel 12:2).

Faith between the Testaments

The trend towards resurrection faith which can be traced in the Old Testament accelerated in Jewish literature between the Testaments. In the Apocrypha one startling passage stands out. It is to be found in Second Maccabees 7 and comes as part of the story of the horrific suffering endured by the Jewish people under the Syrian-Greek ruler Antiochus Epiphanes which sparked off the Maccabean rebellion. This passage concerns seven Jewish brothers and their mother who endure the most gruesome torture, expressing their hope in a future resurrection. The bodily nature of resurrection is stressed here since any future life must involve a recompense for bodily suffering. For example, the mother is made to say to her sons:

> I do not know how you came into being in my womb. It was not I who gave you life and breath, nor I who set in order the elements within each of you. Therefore the Creator of the world, who shaped the beginning of humankind, and devised the origin of all things, will, in his mercy, give life and breath back to you again, since you now forget yourselves for the sake of his laws. (2 Maccabees 7:22,23)

The theologian Hans Küng sums up the implications of this passage in the following remarkable way:

> here emerges the specific character, the distinctive feature of the Jewish expectation of a resurrection, which is so completely different from the Platonic-hellenistic expectations of immortality . . . For . . . what survives is not a human soul by virtue of its own substantial spirituality and divinity; here the whole person is raised by an act of God; by the miracle of a new creation, rooted in God's fidelity to his creature.[7]

Another important development in intertestamental Jewish literature was the rise of the apocalyptic genre. The word *apocalyptic* means 'lifting the veil' and its claim was to reveal the events of the end times and the secrets of the life to come. Often claiming the status of direct vision and revelation, it drew freely on Old Testament imagery and the mythology of other Near

Eastern cultures, in particular Zoroastrianism from Persia.[8] It had an immense influence on the New Testament itself and reached its zenith in the last book of the Bible from whose Greek title, in fact, it derives its name.

Apocalyptic literature is a vast subject in its own right. It incorporates a wide range of ideas and much in it seems to the modern mind to be extremely bizarre. From our point of view, its most important feature is its reaffirmation of the idea of resurrection as the predominant view of life after death in Jewish culture with, sometimes, one specific qualification. Resurrection is not always seen to take place on the continuum of human earthly history. Jewish pessimism about the possibility of justice in this life gave rise to the idea of resurrection taking place outside history, in the heavenly realm.[9]

For now, however, we need only note the comment of one scholar of apocalyptic:

> It is of great significance . . . that they saw survival beyond death in the form of resurrection. Their Hebrew psychology with its belief in the totality of human personality no doubt influenced their thinking in this connection.[10]

The Christian doctrine of resurrection as a future hope based on the historical resurrection of Jesus Christ burst upon the world as something new and startling. We have seen, however, that the *idea* of resurrection which underlies it stretches back over centuries in the Old Testament and Jewish tradition. Before looking at the New Testament, therefore, it might be helpful to summarize the main features of resurrection faith as it had developed so far and to assess it against the criteria of death-transcendence from which we started.

1. Death is a reality. It is something to be feared both as a personal fate and as a denial of the fulfilment of God's loving purposes towards his people.
2. The expectation of future subsistence in Sheol is not a 'hope' of life after death but rather a graphic underscoring of the finality of death itself.
3. Hope therefore consists only in the affirmation of Yahweh's power even over Sheol (death, the grave) itself.
4. Human beings are not viewed as dualisms of body and soul.

The shades in Sheol symbolize the reduction of the whole person in death. No part of a human being is immortal.

5. Life after death, then, can only mean the restoration of the whole person to life.

6. This can only be achieved by the direct re-creative action of God himself. This is true whether resurrection is seen as occurring as an event in human history or, as in some later views, as an event outside the historical continuum.

7. Such a re-creation by God is not merely 'mechanical' but is based on a relationship between God and the person concerned.

8. Resurrection is not only to be seen in terms of human salvation but as a demonstration of the justice of God in the light of the injustice of human life.

The view of life after death which had emerged through the history of Israel is therefore one which takes death seriously; its reality, its horror and its challenge to the meaning of human life are not denied. Nevertheless it offers real hope through its view of the relationship of God to his creation. So far it meets the criteria for a death-transcending orientation. This is the eschatological background to the life of Jesus.

Jesus' Teaching on Resurrection

Jesus himself had things to say about resurrection. It is interesting to note two paradoxical streams of thought in the teaching of Jesus. On the one hand Jesus seems, in many places, very much at home with the common apocalyptic scenario of a final resurrection of all at the end of history, usually followed by a general judgement. This is connected, in Jesus' teaching, with the 'coming of the Son of Man' and is implied, for instance, in the Parable of the Sheep and the Goats in Matthew 25.

There are other passages, however, which seem to indicate a more immediate idea of resurrection in a different realm. The parable of the rich man and Lazarus, for example, seems to show the protagonists receiving their rewards and punishments immediately upon death. Similarly, to the thief on the cross, Jesus says, 'Today you will be with me in Paradise.' To find this tension of timing already in the teaching of Jesus is very interesting and is an issue we shall have to return to.

There is one particular passage which gives us a fascinating insight into Jesus' teaching on resurrection. It is his debate with the Sadducees in Mark 12:18–27. Although Jesus criticized the Pharisees more than any other sect of his time for their hypocritical behaviour, it is interesting to note that, in his eschatological views, he agreed with these inheritors of the tradition of Daniel and the Maccabees in their ongoing dispute with the Sadducees, the party of the temple elite 'who say there is no resurrection' (v. 18).

As Jesus taught in the temple courts of Jerusalem during the final week of his earthly ministry the Sadducees took their turn in challenging Jesus with the famous story of the seven-times married widow. The literal words are significant although somewhat cumbersome in English: 'In the resurrection, when they rise, whose wife will she be? For the seven had her as their wife' (v. 23). Clearly, it is resurrection which is at stake here, not some state of natural immortality. The Greek word for resurrection used throughout the New Testament is a strikingly graphic one: 'anastasis' or 'standing up again'.

The Sadducees, somewhat superciliously, assume resurrection life to be a continuation of this one in all its physical details, including the sexual ones. Hence the evident confusion and therefore the incongruity of the idea of resurrection. There are a number of interesting things about Jesus' reply. He refers to their ignorance of Scripture, where he assumes resurrection to be implied, and to God's power, without which the very idea of resurrection would indeed be impossible.

But a most fascinating detail is the tense of his response, obscured by some English translations which, in their concern for grammatical neatness, miss the point. Although the question was asked in the future tense, Jesus responds in the present: 'When the dead rise, they neither marry nor are married.' (v. 25). Clearly Jesus seems to be indicating something which can be said to be (or not be!) happening right now.

His response also seems to indicate some kind of altered state. The resurrected are 'like the angels in heaven'. This really gives us very little of the flavour of resurrection life. The clue is of little imaginative value unless we know something more about the life-style of angels! The only information we are given here is of a negative character. It presumably indicates that the resurrected are asexual. This solves the problem of the widow's domestic life in heaven but raises more questions. What other differences might there be between resurrected life and this one? Certainly, it seems, human personal relationships are going to be transformed.

Jesus finally sees off his Sadducean opponents with a clever reference to the Pentateuch and the pertinent comment: 'He is not the God of the dead but of the living' (v. 27). But modern readers are left pondering Jesus' vision of resurrection life. This is still resurrection of whole people. But Jesus sees it as taking place immediately upon death in some other place (presumably, like the angels, 'in heaven'). Whatever the resurrected might gain — which is no doubt very great — they lose sexual function and the most intimate of human relationships in terms that we understand in this life.

So far in this chapter, we have not had the state of the bereaved clearly in our sights. We have seen that they are likely to be most helped by a 'death-transcending' orientation and that the idea of resurrection complies with that description. Focusing on this cameo of the teaching of Jesus brings them back into view. Jesus' vision of resurrection still involves loss. If the Sadducees' widow had genuinely loved her seven husbands, then she would have had seven reasons to grieve as they all died one by one. Allowing for the fact that she might meet all seven husbands 'in the resurrection', she will never have the same relationship with any of them.

Jesus clearly believed resurrection life to be greatly superior to this one and so do his followers. We must not trivialize the glory of eternity in the presence of God. However, it is very difficult for us to enter into that glory in our imaginations. As one book puts it the 'many mansions' in the house of our Father 'are not given any domestic flavour'![11] Jesus' teaching clearly indicates that, however great the wonders for which the resurrected exchange the suffering and perplexities of this life, there is something lost at death, or at the death of our loved ones, which will never be regained. There is, however, a positive note even in this negative theme. Jesus grants to the bereaved, alongside hope, a genuine space for grief.

Jesus' Resurrection

During the Easter period of the year this book was written, there erupted a rather unusual degree of public interest in the resurrection of Jesus. A survey published in one Sunday newspaper informed us that fifty percent of the nation believed that Jesus rose from the dead. It is not quite so clear, however, what kind of event such a large number of people claim to believe in. For many years now some theologians have been suggesting that we should take a more 'spiritual' view of the resurrection than that which has been traditionally held in the church through the centuries. In the popular mind such ideas are often associated with names like David Jenkins, once the Bishop of Durham. In fact this kind of thinking goes back much further.

In 1912 B.H. Streeter, a theologian famous for his work on the origins of the gospels, spoke about the resurrection in terms of Jesus' 'personal immortality'.[12] The implication of this phrase is that, although Jesus endured physical death, his real personhood did not die. On the basis of such a Platonic view of Jesus' death, we might say, as Socrates is reported as saying about his own death, that it does not much matter what happened to the body. Imagine then that Jesus' body remained in the tomb; what was it in this case that the disciples are supposed to have seen? Are we to think of such things as hallucinations, autosuggestion and mass-hysteria?

In the 1960s another theologically significant phrase emerged which was to be a milestone in resurrection theory. In a broadcast dialogue subsequently published as a book,[13] the theologian G.W.H. Lampe debated the truth of the resurrection with the philosopher D.H. McKinnon. Attempting to defend the idea of resurrection along spiritual rather than physical lines, Lampe coined the phrase 'objectively real visions'. A later theologian, Paul Badham, had no hesitation in interpreting Streeter's phrase as 'the immortality of his soul' and replaced Lampe's words with the imaginative term 'veridical hallucinations'.[14]

The combination of these two concepts indicates the development of an alternative way of looking at the resurrection of Jesus which dispenses with the need for such intellectually embarrassing details as a revivified corpse. It is a view which has held great appeal for many contemporary theologians and which underlies most attempts to rewrite the story. It can be summarized as follows.

> Although Jesus' body died on the cross, he cannot really be said to have been dead. His immortal soul lived on. From the position of his natural immortality, he desired to demonstrate this 'conquest' of death to his disciples in order to assure them of their own personal survival. This he did by 'appearing' to them in the form of visions which, although they occurred in the minds of the recipients, nevertheless conveyed an objective truth: Jesus was, in reality, still alive.

In all fairness, it must be stressed that people holding this view are not attempting to 'deny' the resurrection of Jesus. Their intention is to recast the doctrine in a form which they find to be intellectually credible. It is even claimed to have biblical justification on the basis of the existence of two alleged strata of resurrection faith in the New Testament.

The first written evidence we have of the resurrection comes in Paul's first letter to the Corinthians. Here Paul speaks of many people, including himself, by whom Jesus 'was seen'. Paul's list of over 500 witnesses is impressive, particularly as many of them were 'still alive' at the time of writing (probably about AD 55). Paul makes no mention of the empty tomb and his account is said to be compatible with the idea of visionary appearances of Jesus which might have no relevance to his physical body.

The secondary stratum is said to begin with the gospel of Mark which, in the shorter ending at least, offers us the empty tomb but no actual appearance of Jesus. The other, later, gospels are said to combine the two kinds of evidence by elaborating the events around the empty tomb and detailing a number of appearances of Jesus. Here the supernatural properties of Jesus' body and the fact that he was not always immediately recognisable is thought to confirm the 'visionary' theory. The following statement is a summary of this view which has since been repeated many times in different words.

> We are therefore presented with two radically different usages of resurrection discourse. The language of the four gospels and of the Acts of the Apostles implies that Jesus' dead body was physically raised from the tomb and was apprehended by the

physical sense organs of the disciples. The language of Paul and 1 Peter suggests that 'Jesus' left his home in the body at death and was raised to a new spiritual existence.[15]

Such a view, however well-intentioned, cannot go unchallenged. From a biblical point of view the argument appears extremely dubious. The powerful testimony of the early church to the empty tomb cannot be dismissed in such a cavalier fashion. There seems little real evidence that Mark was introducing a novel doctrine in his story. The fact that Paul does not mention the tomb is not proof that he had not heard the story that it was empty. He could just as easily have been taking as read something that was axiomatic in early Christian faith. His objective after all in 1 Corinthians 15 was, as we shall see, to demonstrate resurrection faith over other ways of conceiving survival.

Furthermore Luke, who stresses the thoroughness of his research, is at pains to demonstrate the corporeal as well as the supernatural nature of the appearances of Jesus. His narrative, in fact, seems to turn the 'spiritualising' account on its head. It was the first assumption of the disciples that what they were seeing was a 'ghost' or spirit (Luke 24:37). This might indeed tie in with the concept of 'veridical hallucinations'. It was the risen Jesus himself, however, who dispelled these 'doubts' with evidence that he had 'flesh and bones'. Similarly, in John's story it is the wounds of the risen Jesus, indicating the continuity of his physical body with that of the crucified Jesus, which is the conclusive evidence of resurrection both for Thomas and the rest of the disciples.

The direction in which these stories point is that it was the physical body of Jesus, albeit transformed, which for the early Christians demonstrated what resurrection was. Without it (and the complementary evidence of the empty tomb) what they had experienced would not have been the resurrection of Jesus but something else — something, perhaps, which might have corresponded to the theories of some contemporary theologians but to which they could not have given the name of 'anastasis'.

In the context of this book, this trend in thinking about the resurrection of Jesus is very interesting. In the gospel narratives Jesus' fear of death and the ensuing horrors of crucifixion, narrated not morbidly but as matters of fact, indicate that here there is no denial of death. The resurrection stories are completely in line with what we have seen of the concept of resurrection as it developed in Hebraic thought. Death is not avoided but overcome. This occurs not because of a natural condition of immortality but as the result of an exceptional intervention of God on the basis of an intimate personal relationship. The resurrection of Jesus is supremely an act of death-transcendence.

The spiritualising trend in the interpretation of the resurrection can now be seen for what it is, despite its good intention of attempting to save the credibility of resurrection in the modern world. It is a shift into death-denial. Jesus did not really die — nor was he really raised — he simply survived on the basis of his 'personal immortality'. Finally, it has to be said, this view is a form of docetism.

Again, however, we need to examine the implications of this for the bereaved. If to deny death is to impede the grieving process, then it is a serious matter if, at the heart of the Christian faith, there lies a story, not about the conquest of death but about its denial. The resurrection of Jesus is after all, for Christians, the basis and pattern of our hopes for ourselves and our loved ones.

Paul's Teaching on Resurrection

The apostle Paul, some of whose views on both resurrection and the experience of bereavement we have already noted, did not always have an easy time with the early Christian communities which he founded. Perhaps none of them threw up quite so many problems as the church at Corinth. And yet, equally clearly, this was a community for which he held a deep affection. His two letters to the Corinthians, the only record we have of what was clearly a larger and sometimes very painful correspondence, reveal some fascinating insights into the life and practice of early Gentile churches as well as exposing more clearly than anywhere else the pastoral heart of Paul.

They also contain two passages which shed an extraordinary light on the issues we are considering here. Before examining them, there is an important question to consider. Clearly, behind the many problems with which this church was beset, there lay a particular mind-set, represented perhaps by a definite 'party' within the church community but affecting many others also.

What is the unifying factor behind all the many issues with which Paul had to grapple? What exactly was the nature of the opposition which he encountered at Corinth?

Clearly, the doctrine of resurrection was one important issue. Chapter 15 of the first letter, as we have seen, begins with a powerful defence of the historical resurrection of Jesus and, as we shall soon see, goes on to elaborate on the doctrine of resurrection in general. It is interesting to see how this might connect with other issues at stake at Corinth. One commentator, for example, links the Corinthians' attitude to life after death with their extreme supernaturalism and their overemphasis on the more spectacular spiritual gifts.

> In their view, by their reception of the Spirit, and especially the gift of tongues, they had already entered the true 'spirituality' that is to be; already they had begun a form of angelic existence in which the body was unnecessary and unwanted, and would finally be destroyed. Thus for them life in the Spirit meant a final ridding oneself of the body, not because it was evil but because it was inferior and beneath them; the idea that the body would be raised would be anathema.[16]

Another writer links their lack of concern for bodily mortality, which so exasperated Paul, to a view of immortality which discounted the importance of the body. For Paul, however, the way we treat our bodies is important precisely because they are to be raised.[17] In the view of these writers and others, what was happening at Corinth was that the Judaistic roots of Christianity were being challenged in a Greek environment where the predominant view of life and death was a Platonic one.

This is not a recent idea although it has become a more common interpretation in recent years. As long ago as 1933, Karl Barth wrote a fascinating little book, summarising the message of First Corinthians along precisely these lines. He sees chapter 15 and the doctrine of resurrection as the climax towards which the rest of the letter is leading and the interpretative key to the whole. Of Paul's principal opponents at Corinth he says,

> They merely took offence at the Jewish doctrine of the resurrection from the standpoint of the Greek belief in immortality.[18]

So in chapter 15 Paul is strenuously defending the doctrine of resurrection not, as is commonly thought, against those who, like many moderns, have no belief whatever in life after death, but against those who held a view which they believed to be spiritually superior to the Jewish idea of resurrection. Once this idea is accepted, light is immediately shed on the chapter. For example, we see why it is stressed that death has not become for the Christian, as it is for the Platonist, a friend, releasing us from the burden of a troublesome body, but is rather 'the last enemy to be destroyed' (v. 26). We can see also why it is so important for Paul to stress the link between the resurrection (not the 'survival') of Jesus and our own future experience (v. 12–19).

But it must be noted also that here Paul not only *affirms* but also *develops* the concept of bodily resurrection. The alternative to a spiritual and immaterial immortality does not have to be the kind of crude materialism that can be seen, for example, in some of the apocalyptic writers. Paul has moved on from his Pharisaic roots and he demands that the intellectuals at Corinth move on from their Platonic ones. While believing in a bodily resurrection, one does not have to tie oneself to naively materialistic images. The outstanding illustration (an 'analogy' not a 'description' insists Barth) is that of the seed and the plant. Barth comments:

> We suppose seed and plant to be identical; if we did not do so, if we stopped at what is immediately perceptible, here the seed and there the plant, we should have no image of life as a whole, but only of two chaotic heaps, we should then be really fools, we should then have understood nothing of what will happen to the seed and what has happened to the plant. But in the midst thereof, between the two, lies somewhere the critical point where the seed as such, must die, is transferred and transformed wholly into the growing plant. Does this mean perishing? Surely, but just as surely it means growing . . . the zero is at the same time the synthesis of the *plus* and *minus* sides . . . The subject persists, the predicates have become different.[19]

Thus Paul has given us an analogy which at the same time as establishing continuity between the earthly body and the resurrected body also indicates a radical change. This change is marked by death — not an imaginary death, or the death of a part of the person but a genuine 'zero' — and resurrection — not a natural attribute of immortality but a deliberate act of God.

In the same way, Barth takes up Paul's comparison and contrast between man as Adam and Christ:

> We are men of Adam and are to become men of Christ as *corporeal* men, else it would not be true, but as *quite different* corporeal men, otherwise it would also not be true.[20]

Thus Paul introduces the idea of the resurrection body which is a 'spiritual body' because 'flesh and blood cannot inherit the kingdom of God.' So radically necessary is the difference that those still alive at the parousia must go through a similar change even if they escape the trauma of death. In stressing this, Paul underlines something which we have already noted in Jesus' teaching — that resurrection life while retaining personal continuity with this one, is of a very different order. Change, even change to something better, always involves loss and so, like Jesus, Paul, while emphasising the vital importance of resurrection hope, leaves the Christian bereaved something to grieve for.

Once we have Paul's 'immortalist' opponents at Corinth clearly in our sights, another somewhat obscure passage, this time in the second letter to the Corinthians, also becomes clearer. In chapter 5, Paul contemplates death as the destruction of an 'earthly tent-dwelling' (v. 2,3) To replace it, he is expecting 'an eternal house in the heavens'. So far so good. The weak earthly body is to be exchanged for a more substantial resurrection body, much as in the previous letter. In fact the same sort of language is being used (see 1 Corinthians 15:53, 54).

Paul, however, always an individualist in terms of style, mixes his metaphors unashamedly. To the theme of housing he adds that of clothing. We long, he says to be 'clothed with our heavenly dwelling because when we are clothed we shall not be found naked'. The question is the meaning of this state of nakedness. He longs to be 'clothed' or even 'overclothed' with this 'heavenly dwelling' but he emphatically does not want to be 'unclothed'.

The majority view of all this,[21] is that Paul is expressing the hope that the parousia will happen before he dies. That way he would be 'overclothed', transferring directly from an earthly to a heavenly body without having to endure a state of disembodiment between the two (being 'unclothed' or 'naked'). Is Paul, then, expressing belief in a state of temporary disembodiment which he does not relish but which he is prepared to tolerate since, although it means 'moving out of the body' (v. 8) it would also mean 'being at home with the Lord'? This has been described as Paul's 'Catch-22' situation![22]

Clearly this interpretation has its problems. It is admitted, even by those who hold it that it would introduce a new idea in the thinking of Paul, 'catalysed in all probability by controversy with thought of a gnostic kind'.[23] This implies, of course that Paul has allowed himself to be influenced by the thought patterns of his opponents to the extent of accepting belief in an immortal soul which, even if it does not remain in an eternal state of disembodiment, might at least have to endure such a disagreeable state for a period of time.

Furthermore, it is difficult to imagine Paul conceiving a state in which he 'does not wish' to be which can, at the same time, mean being 'at home with the Lord'. In any case, even if Paul's thinking were beginning to move in this direction, there seems to be little reason for stating it here unless he were making some valid point in the context of the problems of Corinth.

Once we remember, however, Paul's critics at Corinth who opposed his doctrine of resurrection from the standpoint of a Platonic belief in immortality — 'the Corinthian Gnostics' as they have been called,[24] — then his words fit into place. The 'nakedness' is not something that Paul expects to experience personally but is a somewhat sarcastic rejection of the state of disembodiment envisaged by the intellectuals of Corinth with Platonic leanings. Unlike them, Paul is saying that he looks forward not to nakedness but to his 'eternal, heavenly dwelling' — a body which can be compared with this one only as a tent might be compared to a solid house.

Immediate Resurrection?

Having accepted this interpretation, however, clearly another question is raised. If Paul expects to move directly from one 'dwelling' to the next, then what has become of his expectation, expressed in the earlier letter and also in writing to the Thessalonians, of a general resurrection of all 'at the last trumpet'? We have seen, in discussing the last passage that the language of an 'interim state' belongs to the logic of immortality rather than to that of resurrection but we are still left with a tension of timing.

Are we, in the vision of the New Testament, to be raised from the dead immediately upon death as an individual and personal event 'in heaven' or will we be raised together when Christ returns? It should not surprise us to find this tension in Paul since we have already encountered it in the teaching of Jesus. Indeed, it seems to be a universal dilemma for anyone who attempts to consistently uphold the doctrine of resurrection.

Anyone who today insists upon the distinction between the biblical doctrine of resurrection and the Platonic concept of the immortality of the soul must recognize themselves as standing in the shadow of Oscar Cullmann who in his famous little book, translated into English in 1958,[25] made the distinction so powerfully and pleaded for a return to authentic biblical categories in this area.

Cullmann contrasted the stories of the death of Socrates and the passion of Jesus and came to the conclusion that:

> The Jewish and Christian interpretation of creation excludes the whole Greek dualism of body and soul . . . The contrast for the Christian is not between body and soul, not between outward form and Idea, but rather between the creation delivered over to death by sin and new creation; between the corruptible, fleshly body and the incorruptible resurrection body.[26]

When Cullmann, came to consider the timing of the resurrection, he found himself struggling with his own argument at this point. He came down firmly on the side of the resurrection of all at the end of time.

> It is not an event which begins with each individual death, but only at the End. It is not a transition from this world to another world . . . rather it is the transition from the present age to the future.[27]

This then led him to attempt to answer the question of what happens 'in between'. Cullmann opted for a kind of doctrine of 'soul-sleep' which not only brought him criticism but led him into an inconsistency which he himself recognized — a 'natural transition' from this life to the next which he had struggled so strenuously to avoid.[28]

This is an extremely complex problem which touches on a number of philosophical issues which, if we stopped to examine them, would take us beyond the scope of this book. A very helpful suggestion, however, is made by the theologian Helmut Thielicke. Thielicke also takes up the idea of sleep, acknowledging it to be a biblical metaphor for death — but only a metaphor. The real solution is to be found by considering that death takes us out of the time continuum in which this life is lived.

> the metaphor of sleep indicates that the dead are called out of time (as those who sleep lose a sense of time in dreams). Thus the interval between dying and the resurrection at the last day no longer presents a problem of time . . . The resurrection at the end is, then, an awakening out of sleep. The removal of a sense of time means for those who are awakened that the long night of death is reduced to a mathematical point, and they are thus summoned out of completed life.[29]

On this view, a person who dies ceases to exist for those who survive him in this life. It is not that he is 'somewhere else' as if he had gone to another country where there is no means of communication with this one but where he can nevertheless be imagined as existing in parallel with his survivors. He is dead and will not live again until the resurrection at the end of time which we all await.

From the point of view of his own experience, however, there is no 'time' between his death and resurrection since being dead takes one out of the experience of time. Thielicke compares this experience to awakening out of sleep. Perhaps a more vivid comparison might be someone recovering from an anaesthetic in which consciousness has been totally lost: it is as if one had temporarily ceased to exist. These are only subjective analogies, however. In death there is no sleeper, no 'person' still breathing on the operating table. There is someone who has died and who will be raised to life again by the power of God.

The person who dies in resurrection faith does not die trusting that his immortal soul will continue to live once his physical body has stopped functioning. Such a person dies, like Jesus, abandoning himself in trust and hope 'to the one who could save him out of death' (Hebrews 5:7).

Resurrection and the Bereaved

As we have considered the biblical doctrine of resurrection, a number of features have emerged which are of great importance for the experience of the bereaved. It might be helpful to summarize them here:

(1)   Death is seen as a reality. It affects the whole person.
(2)   Because resurrection takes place at the end of time, for the bereaved, their loved ones are totally unavailable. In an important sense, it can be said that they do not exist.
(3)   In the teaching of both Jesus and Paul resurrection is seen as being raised to a totally different order of life.
(4)   One important aspect of this difference is a transformation of human relationships.

These elements might be seen as the 'negative' aspects of the doctrine of resurrection for the bereaved. They present a real loss and something for which to genuinely grieve. Nevertheless the New Testament also maintains that:

(5)   Resurrection is assured on the basis of analogy with the resurrection of Jesus.
(6)   Resurrection on this basis is of the whole person — including a transformed body. As Jesus was recognized by his disciples so we might expect to recognize each other.
(7)   For the dead themselves there is no 'time' between death and resurrection. The 'dead in Christ' are 'with the Lord'.
(8)   Resurrection faith thus offers to the bereaved a hope for the future. Hope is a powerful resource for coping but must be sharply distinguished from the kind of comfort which maintains that it is 'all right' in the present.

The combination of these features eminently qualifies the doctrine of resurrection as a 'death-transcending' idea in terms of the categories with which we began this chapter. It does not deny the reality of death. Nor does it abandon hope in the face of such a reality. It gives to the bereaved a source of grief and a resource of hope to sustain them through it.

Chapter 7

IMMORTALITY AND THE DENIAL OF DEATH

In 1991, a survey was conducted into what its author called the 'combinatorial explosion in theories of mind' that had taken place during the 1980s. In all the vast array of philosophical and psychological thinking about what the human mind is and how it functions, she found only one common element. It was this: 'all find dualism implausible'.[1] What this means is that, in philosophical and scientific circles, the idea that human beings are made up of a soul (or mind) and body which can be separated one from the other is distinctly outmoded. Rather, thinking people are more likely to consider themselves today as an inseparable combination of body and mind or soul. This, of course, was not a 'discovery' of the '80s but a trend that had been developing throughout the century.

In such an intellectual climate, we might expect to find the Platonic idea of the immortality of the soul losing ground to the sort of thinking about death and resurrection which was outlined in the last chapter. This would appear not only to comply more easily with the historical development of hope for life beyond death in the Bible but also to fit much more neatly into the way we are encouraged to think about the nature of human beings. It turns out that, as one writer put it: 'Resurrection of the Body is not only more biblical than Immortality of the Soul, it also makes better sense.'[2]

This is not always how the situation is seen. One famous philosopher of religion notes this fact with some surprise:

> The prevailing view of man among both contemporary scientists and Western philosophers is that he is an indissoluble psycho-

spiritual unity . . . Against this background of thought, the specifically Christian and Jewish belief in the resurrection of the body, in contrast to the hellenic idea of the survival of a disembodied soul, might be expected to have attracted more attention than it has.[3]

Indeed, if human beings are a psychosomatic unity it would appear that the only possible way in which life after death could be contemplated would have to be in terms of a resurrection or re-creation in some form of the whole person. The paradoxical fact, however, is that, in parallel with the trend in scientific and philosophical thinking towards a more 'monistic' view of human nature, most popular and much theological thinking about life after death has assumed that this can best be thought of in terms of a separation of soul and body.

The results of this include the way in which thinking about the resurrection of Jesus has, as we have seen, been increasingly 'spiritualized' in the past few decades. It is also evidenced in much thinking about life after death in a general way. Thus, we find it being asserted that 'rational belief in a future life depends upon the validity of the concept of the soul'[4] and that 'the belief in survival hinges on a dualism of mind and body'.[5] Why, in this generation of all generations, should an anthropology which can be shown to be both unbiblical and scientifically outmoded, be clung to so tenaciously by Christians wanting to demonstrate the possibility of life after death?

One way of answering that question is to begin with the categories of attitudes towards death outlined in the last chapter. It has been argued that the Christian doctrine of resurrection is an authentically *death-transcending* orientation: that is, that it does not deny the reality of death but holds out a hope beyond it. We have also seen that such a position is constantly under siege from both *death-accepting* and *death-denying* ideas. *Death-accepting* ideas would seem to be evident enough in our society in the kind of secular thinking that sees death as the end of all possible conscious existence. It may seem contradictory, therefore, to say that we live in a *death-denying* age. This, however, is what many people would claim to be profoundly true and, moreover, it is the denial of death which poses a much more subtle threat to Christian thinking.

If we wish to see why it is that the Platonic idea of the immortality of the soul retains such great seductive appeal for so many in our so-called scientific age, then we must remember that it has proved historically to be the most successful form of death-denial in Western thinking — and it is a way of denying the force and reality of death that our secular age craves. If this is true, we may wonder why it is that so many today find the need to deny death so compelling. To answer this question we must first look at the human psyche and then examine some of the death-denying forces in our contemporary society.

The Denial of Death

What exactly does it mean to deny death? Is it simply a bad habit that individuals or societies fall into from time to time, which can be easily corrected by honest thinking? It would appear not to be so easy. Thinking about human attitudes to death was revolutionized by the appearance in 1973 of a book by Ernest Becker called *The Denial of Death.*[6] Becker was a psychoanalytical thinker who took some important Freudian concepts and developed them in a new and surprising way. His ideas are so relevant to this discussion and take us so much further into an understanding of what it means to deny death that it is worth attempting to summarize the main features of his argument.

Becker's fundamental thesis is that, 'behind the sense of insecurity in the face of danger, behind the sense of discouragement and depression, there always lurks the basic fear of death.' Not only so, but this same fear 'lies behind all normal functioning which aims at self-preservation' and because it cannot consciously be present in our functioning there has to be a 'constant psychological effort to keep the lid on . . . Therefore in normal times we move about actually without ever believing in our own death.'[7] Thus, according to Becker, the denial of death is a basic feature of human life. It is the way we cope with what would be an intolerable fear if we remained constantly conscious of it.

This repression, according to Becker, begins early in childhood and accounts for the apparent disappearance of the fear of death in those with a 'favoured upbringing'. The denial of death is thus on the psychoanalytic definition the repression of the fear of death which all of us carry from early childhood. For

Becker the child's fundamental problem is in reconciling his death-prone animal nature with his sense of 'symbolic identity and self-consciousness'. The human character which results and with which the child learns to face the world is in fact a 'Pyrrhic victory' because it 'hides an inner defeat' in terms of the 'toll that his pretence of sanity takes'.[8]

Becker then takes several Freudian ideas which in their conception had a sexual orientation and recasts them in the mould of his denial-of-death theory.[9] He goes to great lengths to discuss why an intellect as brilliant as Freud's should have underestimated the importance of the fear of death and attributed so much to sexuality, and also to show how much of what classic psychoanalytic theory missed can be found in Kierkegaard, who, as an existentialist theologian, faced the reality of his own fear of death.[10] Freud, in fact, had repressed his own fear of death very successfully!

More important here, however, is the essential dilemma which emerges from this concept of the denial of death as a necessary repression common to all humanity. On the one hand our repression of the fear of death is a 'neurotic structure' which prevents our discovering 'our authentic self: what we really are without sham, without disguise, without defenses against fear'.[11] On the other hand the question has to be asked, 'What exactly would it mean on this earth to be wholly unrepressed, to live in full bodily and psychic expansiveness? It can only mean to be reborn into madness.'[12]

Becker's answer to his own question takes an unexpected turn when he deals with the subject of religion. Religion in general and Christianity in particular seem to him to provide the best possible solution to the dilemma.

> Religion then, gives the possibility of heroic victory in freedom and solves the problem of human dignity at its highest level. The two ontological motives of the human condition are both met: the need to surrender oneself in full to the rest of nature, to become a part of it by laying down one's whole existence to some higher meaning; and the need to expand oneself as an individual heroic personality. Finally religion alone gives hope because it holds open the dimension of the unknown and the unknowable.[13]

Thus for Becker, a religious view of death, far from being another form of denial, can in fact be the most successful, if not the only, way to cope with the reality of death with at least a minimum of repression and without madness. This validation of religion does not go unqualified. He criticizes, for example, what he calls a 'transference' of power onto religious hero figures. Nevertheless, he concludes that, in terms of allowing human beings to cope with the reality of death, 'Christianity, on all the things we have listed, stands high, perhaps even highest in some vital ways'.[14]

Becker's thesis is relevant in two important ways to the subject of this book. First, he shows us why the denial of death holds such universal appeal. It is something deeply embedded in the human psyche from early childhood. Secondly, he raises the possibility that Christianity may hold a unique way of allowing human beings to face their own death by offering a form of transcendence that need not involve denial.

Becker, of course, does not analyse what form this transcendence might take from a theological point of view. Much less is his writing a polemic for traditional Christianity. Nevertheless, his own position is an interesting one. He died a few months after writing his famous book. In an interview on his deathbed he clarified where he stood in relation to religion:

> [I] feel a great sense of relief and trust that eggs are not hatched in vain. Beyond accident and contingency and terror and death there is a meaning that redeems, redeems not necessarily in personal immortality or anything like that but a redemption that makes it good somehow. And that is enough . . . I think it is very hard for secular man to die.[15]

The Modernisation of Dying

Ernest Becker was, of course, writing from a psychoanalytical viewpoint that not all Christians might feel sympathetic towards. Nevertheless, the central truth of what he is saying is evident enough to anyone: the denial of death is something that affects all human beings. It is not peculiar to particular individuals, ages or cultures but is rather a commonplace of humanity. It is the way all human beings deal with our fear of annihilation.

It might still be true, however, that some societies are more death-denying than others. The claim that our own period of Western culture has a particularly death-denying tendency can be demonstrated in two main areas which we might call *the clinical care of the dying* and *the disposal of the dead.*

In previous generations dying was a family or a community affair. Except in cases of accidents or sudden illness, people died at home, often surrounded in their last days and hours by family and friends. It was members of the family, often supported by neighbours, who cared for the dying and 'laid out' the dead. People lived close to death and most people witnessed dying as a part of life. In such a context, it was perhaps easier to come to terms with the reality of death and to accept the unpalatable truth of one's own mortality.

Over the last few decades, however, there has occurred, in the Western world, a process which has been called the 'modernisation of dying.'[16] It stems largely from the very success of medical science. More and more life-threatening illnesses have come under control and we are living longer. For this our generation has to be grateful. As with many medical advances, however, there are side-effects. One is that now most people die in hospitals or in institutions of one kind or another. A close relative — a husband or wife, son or daughter, for example — may or may not be at the bedside but, in most cases, the process of dying and the moment of death have become very private affairs. The truth of death is tucked away behind hospital blinds. Most people do not encounter death at close hand until relatively late in life.

A further corollary of medical success is that if the cure of a patient who might previously have died is the measure of clinical success, then the death of a patient is a failure. This increases the pressure in hospitals for death to be hidden away. Its reality is accepted only as a 'last resort when all else fails'.[17]

It is true, of course, that the hospice movement pioneered by Dame Cicely Saunders, the founder of St. Christopher's Hospice in London, has done great work in raising awareness of the needs of dying patients and 'humanizing' the process of dying. In hospices in many parts of the country, dying people have discovered staff who still consider them of value even when all hope for their survival has gone. Nevertheless, this success has been so noteworthy precisely because it runs counter to the contemporary trend. Even in this country, where the hospice movement began, hospice care is only available to a small percentage of the dying.

For most people in our society, for most of their lives, death is something which happens in special places — hospitals, hospices, nursing homes — removed from the mainstream of normal life. When it happens to people we know — even in relative old age — it is viewed as the ultimate failure of the medical profession. And all this comes on top of our human tendency to suppress our own fear of death by psychological denial. Little wonder, then, that we find the reality of death a difficult thing to face.

After the medical professions have 'failed':

> Disposal of the body is handed over to other professionals, and the grief counselling turned over to the religious professionals.[18]

The second area in which our age demonstrates its death-denying tendency is in terms of what happens after a person dies. In the 1960s two important studies, one American and one British, called for a re-examination of the way in which we were beginning to handle the disposal of our dead and the public mourning customs which surround it. Although, at the time, both of these were applauded, there seems to be little evidence that the trends they were deploring have been reversed. Indeed, some of these trends have now become so commonplace that we take them for granted.

The first study was Jessica Mitford's scathing but surprisingly entertaining exposé of the American funeral industry *The American Way of Death*. The villains of the piece for Mitford are the funeral directors who take upon themselves a lucrative and all-embracing role in relation to death, removing the reality of it as far as possible from the bereaved:

> He has relieved the family of every detail, he has revamped the corpse to look like a living doll, he has arranged for it to nap for a few days in a slumber room, he has put on a well oiled performance in which the concept of *death* has played no part whatsoever — unless it was inconsiderately mentioned by the clergyman who conducted the religious service.[19]

Mitford is at pains to point out that most British funeral directors are not in the same mould as their American counterparts.[20] Certainly the open coffin is usually, in this country, reserved for close family and is not normally, as in the United States, open at the funeral service. Some people, however, would see the

increase in cremations as opposed to burials, which has undoubt-
edly become a part of the scene in this country, as part of the
tendency to 'sanitize' death and avoid facing its reality in a
funeral service. One Christian writer memorably describes the
crematorium as 'a Municipal Euphemism, avoidance on the
rates'![21]

Shortly after Mitford's book appeared, Geoffrey Gorer wrote
his influential *Death, Grief and Mourning in Contemporary
Britain*.[22] In this survey he deplored the demise in our society
of accepted social mourning customs. Where such 'time-limited'
customs prevail, he claimed, the bereaved are given permission
and even encouraged to grieve but their grief has an expected
end-point. A lack of such customs, on the other hand, leaves
bereaved people and their friends bewildered, not knowing how
to behave towards one another. Gorer blamed the decline of
religious values in our society and pleaded for some other ways
of marking the reality of death in a social context.

The Denial of Death by Christians

Mitford and Gorer warned, at a fairly early stage in the process,
of trends which have only become more marked in recent
decades: funeral services are conducted increasingly in ways
which avoid the real truth that someone has died; accepted social
customs surrounding the period after a death have declined,
leaving people increasingly embarrassed and confused about the
fact of death. Interestingly, both these writers regard religion as
having the potential to introduce a note of reality in the midst of
this process.

Indeed Christian voices have been raised in protest from time
to time against this increasingly institutionalized attitude to
death. However, the position of the Christian church in relation
to funeral rites is a complicated one. Andrew Walker, for example
deplores this process which he sees as part of the secularisation
of society and calls on Christians to resist. However he himself
recognizes that in this area 'priests and pastors are caught in a
trap' because the area of death is the 'one monopoly left to the
church in modernity'. The reason for this is one of default: 'Death
is the unforgivable sin of modernity, and the modern world will
have nothing to do with her.' The 'religious professional' there-

fore is in danger of being simply a 'cog in the death machine'.[23]

In this situation Christianity is faced with a problem. We have seen that, inherent in Christianity itself, there is a tendency to slip into death-denial. In the modern world there is even greater pressure for it to collaborate with a prevailing cultural trend in the same direction. It can easily become the 'chaplain' to the contemporary scene offering a thin veneer of religious comfort to assist in the process of avoidance. The funeral liturgy itself can easily 'accommodate itself to our death-denying culture'[24] and thus fail the bereaved.

It is interesting but rather worrying to see the way in which the trends in contemporary society which have been noted are reflected in popular Christian culture. We have seen that the denial of death manifests itself in our society in the way that death is seen from a medical perspective and the way in which we perceive and practise the disposal of our dead. Both of these tendencies have an equivalent in what has become the Christian subculture.

The first is to be seen in the context of the Christian healing ministry. While this is to be welcomed as a recognition of the relevance of faith to the whole of life including the physical body, it oversteps its boundaries when it becomes assumed, or is even taught, that supernatural physical healing is an almost automatic right of the Christian believer. This kind of approach has, however, proved to be extremely popular in some circles in recent years. Where death occurs after much prayer, anointing and the laying on of hands, it can become the spiritual equivalent of a medical 'failure'. Often, under these conditions, the approach of death is heavily denied by both the dying persons and their loved ones. When it has happened, it is as far as possible ignored and the grieving process minimized.

Ray Anderson, who taught at Fuller Theological Seminary at the same time that John Wimber held his seminars on 'power healing' there, was acutely aware of the problem:

> Some have interpreted the promise to mean that every person has a right to expect that God will heal the one who prays in faith. Stories of apparently miraculous healing are used to support this expectation. This poses a problem: how do we uphold the faith of the dying person in the light of these promises and these expectations?[25]

Anderson, who has no wish to deny the possibility of supernatural healing, finds support in Bonhoeffer's distinction between ultimate and penultimate eschatological reality. Healings which do occur are to be seen as 'sacraments of the resurrection' and therefore 'the healing of one person is not a "truth" which condemns others who are not healed. The healing of the one is a sacrament of that truth which holds good for all.'[26] This is Anderson's response to the issue and is one that can be very helpful. The point is, however, that if the church is really to proclaim the possibility of healing through prayer, it must find ways of doing so which equally support the dying and bereaved and which do not portray their 'non-healing' as a failure of faith.

The second reflection in the church of the secular tendency to death-denial is to be seen in relation to the funeral service itself. Increasingly, there is pressure upon ministers taking funerals for Christian families to avoid the realities of loss and grief in the funeral service. This is sometimes demonstrated in the title of the service which could well be referred to as a thanksgiving for or even a celebration of the person's life. Sometimes the most tragic deaths are dealt with publicly in a way that leaves no space for the expression of grief of shattered loved ones or bewildered friends. The spirit of Aristeides, it seems, is still with us!

Of course, one element in a funeral service will be a sense of gratitude to God for a person's life. Where celebration becomes the major focus of a funeral service, however, the service loses its potential of helping the grieving accept the reality of their loss in the context of the worship of God. Grief then becomes split off from those emotions which can openly be expressed in God's presence. The bereaved have been failed and, paradoxically, deprived of their comfort in God.

Secular Immortalism

We live in a death-denying culture — one in which both the care of the dying and the disposal of the dead are done in a way designed to minimize the impact of the fact of death itself. This attitude is abroad in our secular culture and is reflected in the church. To return then to the paradox with which this chapter began, it now seems less surprising that, despite the Bible and contemporary scientific thinking, people should choose a theology of death which also denies its reality. How comforting to be assured that the horror which we hide behind curtains in the hospital or the crematorium is really an illusion. People do not really die — they 'pass on' or simply 'go' leaving the empty shell of a body. There is thus no real problem; no need to grieve. This is the rationale of immortality.

As we have seen, the idea of the natural immortality of the soul has pervaded our culture through Augustinian Christianity which has characterized the Western church for many centuries, surviving on both sides of the Reformation divide, alive today in Evangelical as much as Catholic spirituality. In the Western world when someone speaks about life after death, the form of this which most people would envisage is the survival of an immortal, immaterial soul which lives on after the body has ceased to function. In picturing this kind of postmortem existence, whether believed in or not, there would be a general impression that this is the Christian view. It may be seen as one of the legacies of Christianity to our post-Christian society.

Immortality, if it is to survive in today's world, however, must find other ways of expressing itself. There are three principal forms which the idea of immortality has taken on once loosened from its Christian moorings.

Reincarnation

There has been a revival of interest in the idea of reincarnation. This is often attributed to the fascination of the Western mind with Eastern religions, particularly Buddhism, since the 1960s. The appeal of reincarnation to the contemporary Western mind, however, is a natural one. Once a belief in an immaterial soul surviving the body at death is firmly established and this is freed from any Christian scruples about the uniqueness of each earthly life, it is quite predictable that this will lead on to the possibility of further embodiments. Indeed, in the minds of many people, this may not seem totally incongruous with Christianity itself. One survey claimed to demonstrate that 'virtually as many Anglicans believe in reincarnation as believe in heaven and hell.'[27] If such a statistic means anything, it shows not only that the idea is prevalent in Britain but that it is viewed by many who hold it as consistent with what is perceived as Christian teaching.

In fact, the concepts of immortality of the soul and of reincarnation have gone together from the beginning. In Plato's *Republic*, as we have seen, the fate of each soul after its thousand year period of purification was to choose for itself, in a prescribed order, a new body, either human or animal. The idea was not totally ruled out of court by some of the more hellenistically minded church fathers like Origen.

In the modern world the idea received fresh impetus as a result of the publication of a collection of supposed evidence for reincarnation by Ian Stevenson[28] which has sparked off a recent philosophical debate about the plausibility of the idea.[29] In the popular mind, however, the possibility that we have 'been here before' or that our disembodied souls will find another embodiment in a later life is well established.

Spiritualism

If departed souls have not found a subsequent embodiment but remain somewhere in immaterial form, then the next possibility is that we might find a way of communicating with them. Spiritualism in its classic modern form began as a late nineteenth century phenomenon arising paradoxically in a period of increasing scientific certainties and growing scepticism about transcendental matters. Its origin is usually associated with the Fox sisters in America.

Its vision of the afterlife does not appeal to everyone and has been described as 'the drab offerings of the continuation of lower-middle-class Brighton life to eternity'![30] However the undoubted appeal of spiritualism to many is the fact that the possibility of actually communicating with the disembodied spirits of the dead seems to offer a certainty about the truth and nature of life after death not to be found in other religious approaches. So, for example, one spiritualistic writer, in a book confidently entitled *What Happens when you Die?* affirms 'In the present work I describe in . . . detail what actually happens to a person when he dies, . . . the evidence being derived not only from the still living, but also from the dead through mediumistic communications.'[31]

Classic spiritualism has a rather dated feel about it, but more recently a revamped version of the concept has enjoyed renewed prestige as a phenomenon of the New Age Movement where the term used for communication with the dead is 'channelling' as experienced most famously by the actress Shirley Maclaine.[32] The fact is that once the idea of a naturally immortal soul is firmly established, it is almost a normal progression to go on to explore methods of communication between embodied and disembodied minds and thus to discover what the future life is like.

There is also, of course, the tantalizing possibility that this route might produce proof that such a thing as life after death exists. Even a respectable religious philosopher, H.D. Lewis, succumbed to this. He pleaded that what he calls 'psychic research' should not be treated contemptuously by religious persons. 'Proof' by this means would, he said, be 'momentous'.[33] A more adventurous Christian dualist like Martin Israel can make the astounding affirmation that, 'it is probable that the trend of postmortem existence has been fairly accurately charted by spiritualism.'[34]

Near-Death Experiences

Perhaps the most authentically modern phenomenon of 'secular immortalism' is the recent flurry of interest in what are called 'near-death' or even 'after-death' experiences. A number of people claim to have 'died' and 'left the body' and to have actually experienced a transcendent or disembodied state before 'returning' to resume bodily life. A collection of such stories compiled by Raymond Moody, for example, has proved extremely popular.[35] If this is a correct interpretation of what has happened to such people, it becomes a powerful argument in favour of the idea of an immortal soul. Again, the ancestry of this idea can be seen as stretching back to Plato.[36]

What, then, are we to make of such claims? Many Christians warm to the idea that they are reliable, seeing them as evidence of a life beyond this one. If this were so, however, we should have to ask what kind of life these experiences would be giving evidence of. The philosopher Christopher Cherry has examined the nature of these claims closely. His conclusion is that 'such extrapolations to a postmortem state are, sad to say, wholly illicit'. What is being described, he maintains, is some kind of mental state in this life. He comments that the conclusion that they relate to an after-death experience is 'a fascinating echo of the view that everyone is really convinced of his own immortality.'[37]

It would seem that the evidence of such experiences can be looked at in two ways. Convinced dualists will see such things as proof of what they already believe. It could, however, also be argued that belief in disembodied souls prejudices the interpretation of these phenomena. In other words, it is because a belief in immortal souls is latent in the belief-systems of our culture that people interpret such experiences as evidence of life after death, rather than as the processes of a human mind convinced that death is near. The idea of immortality itself, therefore, is the parent rather than the offspring of this interpretation.

The Problem with Denial

The idea of the immortality of the soul chimes with the death-denying tendency of our age and retains its popularity even in a so-called secular society. Where it is not linked specifically with a Christian faith it can easily express itself in other forms such as belief in reincarnation, spiritualism or claims to after-death experiences. Indeed, these things can be seen also to affect the thinking of Christians and, as we shall see, their interpretations of bereavement experiences.

Belief in immortality is very attractive in bereavement. It tells the grieving person that the essential 'part' of their loved one has not really died. What is left is 'just a shell'; the 'real' person is in a 'better place'. Such language is not too far removed from Neoplatonic talk about the body as a 'tomb' or a 'prison'.[38] It may well lead to the conclusion that grief is not really an appropriate feeling. The correct response ought to be to rejoice that the deceased is now 'free'. Now all of this may well be what the bereaved would like to hear. Any way out of the pain being experienced is to be welcomed. Emotional efforts are often made to bring the feelings in line with this belief.

This idea is even more seductive to someone caring for a bereaved person. For the helper watching someone else's pain, the first reaction is often to relieve it. To persuade the bereaved of the truth of immortality is in such circumstances a strong temptation. It is to argue that the loved one is not really dead at all. It is to attempt to alleviate the pain by claiming that death has not really taken place. It is to claim that *there is no need to grieve!*

To cling to immortality in such circumstances, however, raises a number of problems. The first is the incongruity between belief and experience. In many cases the bereaved person believes that death is an illusion. The life of the deceased has continued in an uninterrupted fashion. Only the body is left which is 'not him'. What she feels, however, is the full nihilistic impact of death. To the experience of the bereaved the beloved has ceased to exist. Death is real and the loved one is really lost to her. Grief is an experience which has to be felt or else suppressed with the greatest of emotional effort.

To believe in immortality at the point of bereavement and to maintain that belief in the face of grief is to deny death itself. To be given the opportunity to indulge in denial at this point is superficially comforting but cannot be achieved without great emotional and psychological cost. Reality itself, as experienced by the bereaved person, is having to be denied.

There is a second layer of difficulty, particularly for the deeply convinced Christian, who understands immortality to be a part of his faith. He must feel strongly the inappropriateness of his experience to what he believes to be true. The feeling of grief thus becomes a cause for guilt. When this happens, faith in God, which could be a source of strength, actually becomes an aggravation to the pain already being endured. God is not uncommonly perceived as judging the bereaved for 'wrong' feelings. A sense of neurotic guilt thus increases the pain while removing a resource for support in enduring it.

Thirdly, there is the effect of denial upon the grieving process. This is something to be looked at in the next part of the book. By examining the contemporary understanding of bereavement from a psychological perspective, we shall begin to see just how damaging to the course of grief is a belief system which has at its core the denial of death.

PART IV
Psychology and the Tasks of Grieving

Chapter 8

WHAT IS GRIEF?

On a night in 1943 a disaster occurred in Boston, Massachusetts. Following a football match in the city between the university teams of Harvard and Yale, young people crammed into a night club known as the *Cocoanut Grove*. In the midst of the celebrations fire broke out resulting in a colossal loss of life. This disaster is of great importance in our understanding of grief because a psychiatrist called E. Lindemann dedicated himself to the care and study of 101 bereaved relatives of those who had died and subsequently published his findings in the *American Journal of Psychiatry*.[1]

Although no doubt moved by compassion for the victims of this catastrophe, Lindemann had scientific reasons for wanting to study the effects of bereavement. He had been involved in a psychological study of patients suffering from ulcerative colitis. There seemed to be no known physical cause for this illness and Lindemann had been seeking to discover if there might be a psychological one. Nine months before the *Coconut Grove* disaster he had reported that 'loss of security, especially the loss of another person of emotional significance, is frequently encountered as the crisis in human relationships which preceded the onset of the illness.'[2] Thus Lindemann had established a link between bereavement and physical illness. His study of the bereaved victims of the *Coconut Grove* was to take him even further.

Laying the Foundations

Freud

Lindemann was not the first to take an interest in bereavement from a psychiatric point of view. He was, in fact standing in a tradition stretching back to Sigmund Freud. In 1917 Freud had published a paper called *Mourning and Melancholia*.[3] He had, however, little interest in the process of grief as such. His primary interest was in what he called 'melancholia' but which we today would call 'depression'. The phenomenon of grief was for him a sort of model to help in the understanding of this. In itself, grief was only of real interest when it became pathological.

For Freud,

> 'mourning' is the process by which libido (sexual energy) is withdrawn from a love object . . . until each memory that bound the libido to it has been brought up and 'hypercathected'.[4]

It is to describe this process that Freud coined the extremely influential term, 'grief-work'. Both grief and depression were, according to Freud, reactions to loss and manifested similar symptoms. The major difference was the element of self-reproach and consequent lack of self-esteem which Freud believed to be absent from healthy grief. Where a relationship has been ambivalent, he believed, libido is sometimes withdrawn from the lost loved one only to be attached to the bereaved's own ego. A process of identification occurs which leads to self-reproach.

Without intending to, perhaps, Freud had set a ball rolling which was going to gather momentum throughout the century. Almost coincidentally he had posited a process of healthy grief, he had introduced the idea of identification as a phenomenon within grief and had warned of the effects upon the grieving process of an ambivalent relationship, all of which were to prove of interest to later theorists. He had also aroused interest in tracing the borderline between normal and pathological grief.

Later advances in the understanding of bereavement were to arise in the context of Freudian psychoanalytic theory. For example, in 1937 Helene Deutsch[5] noted that experiences of bereavement in childhood could affect a person's subsequent psychological development. She also drew attention to the phenomenon of the absence of conscious grieving which I shall refer to in the next chapter. In 1940 Melanie Klein[6] made an important connection between early childhood experiences of bereavement and later adult reactions to loss. She was also the first to point out the importance of the role of family and friends in helping people to recovery after suffering pathological reactions to loss.

Lindemann

All these developments in the first half of the century came about in a context in which interest lay not so much in the process of grief as a valid area of enquiry in itself, but in its contribution to psychiatric illness. As a later bereavement theorist put it, 'In the history of psychoanalytic thought the study of grief and mourning has usually been approached by way of the study of depressive illness in adults'.[7] This was the tradition in which Lindemann stood as he began his work with the *Cocoanut Grove* victims.

Like those who had gone before him, Lindemann noted a number of types of distorted reactions in unresolved grief: excessive activity with no sense of loss; psychosomatic symptoms similar to those of the deceased; alterations in relationships; extreme hostility towards people associated with the death; behaviour resembling a schizophrenic pattern; severe depression with a risk of suicide.

The most influential feature of Lindemann's work was his stress on the importance of establishing an account of the normal process of grief against which pathological reactions can be measured. These latter, he maintained, are to be seen, not as different kinds of grief but as exaggerations or distortions of a normal process. This is recognized by later writers to be an extremely important principle to which the whole subsequent course of bereavement study owes a debt.[8] Most important for the subject of this book, however, is the chief reason that Lindemann gives for the distortion of normal processes that causes grief to go wrong:

> One of the biggest obstacles to this ('grief-work') seems to be the fact that many patients try to avoid the intense distress connected with the grief experience and to avoid the emotion necessary for it.[9]

The foundation which Lindemann laid and on which subsequent bereavement study has been built can therefore be summarized as follows:

(1) Grief has a 'normal' course or process which is worthy of study in its own right and which, if unhindered by complicating psychological or circumstantial factors, will eventually result in a satisfactory outcome.

(2) Normal and pathological grief are not different kinds of grief. Pathological grief is rather a distorted or exaggerated form of the normal process.

(3) One of the principal reasons for the occurrence of these distortions or exaggerations is the avoidance of grief-work on the part of the bereaved sufferer.

The first of these points will be the subject of the rest of this chapter as we look in greater detail at what 'normal' grief is like. The second two will be dealt with in the next chapter where we shall consider the ways in which grief can become complicated and relate this to the theological issues that have already been raised in this book.

How then is the normal process of grief to be described? Lindemann took up Freud's model of grief-work. This is a metaphor often adopted in contemporary bereavement literature.[10] Other models frequently employed are a process of healing,[11] of change[12] or of adjustment to 'object loss'.[13] What all these paradigms have in common is that they describe an unpleasant and often very painful process.

John Bowlby, to whose work I shall be referring shortly, gives a graphic description of the best possible prognosis for the course of a bereavement. He sets out the kind of experience that the most favoured individual is likely to pass through in his bereavement.

> On being confronted with the loss of someone close to him such a person will not be spared grief; on the contrary he may grieve deeply and on occasion, perhaps, be intensely angry . . . Since he will not be afraid of intense and unmet desires for love from the person lost, he will let himself be swept by pangs of grief; and tearful expressions of yearning and distress will come naturally.[14]

It must be remembered that what is being described here is not pathological grief or grief gone wrong but the healthiest possible response to the loss of a loved one through death. It is evident that, for even the best disposed individual, it is only through a process involving much suffering that the bereaved can arrive at a resolution of her loss.

Kübler-Ross

After Lindemann, the next influential development in the conceptualisation of the process of bereavement came not from the study of bereavement itself but from the observation of the experiences of the dying. The research of Elisabeth Kübler-Ross with dying patients has contributed greatly to the beginning of a dispelling of the taboo on death and grief as subjects for discussion. In her book *On Death and Dying*,[15] she described the emotions of people who know that they are shortly about to die in terms of a series of stages. She maintained that, where there is enough time and provided that patients are courageous enough to face their own feelings, they will typically pass through a sequence of five stages. These are: (1) denial and isolation; (2) anger; (3) bargaining; (4) depression; (5) acceptance.

As we shall see, these stages are similar, but not identical to, the kind of list normally set out in the study of bereavement. The importance of Kübler-Ross's contribution lies in the very idea of a sequence of stages through which individuals pass in working towards a sense of resolution of their loss. The concept has been most helpful in providing a framework for the understanding of bereavement in subsequent years. It has become almost universally accepted but sometimes with important qualifications. Its danger lies in a rigid expectation of uniformity in dying and bereaved people. Colin Murray Parkes, for example, calls for flexibility in interpreting the stages. They are not to be considered as watertight compartments but as 'a succession of clinical pictures which blend into and replace one another' until eventual reorganisation takes place.[16]

Attachment Theory

I have already referred to the names of the two people whose work dominates the contemporary psychological understanding of bereavement. They are John Bowlby and Colin Murray Parkes. Both of these writers approach the subject from the perspective of psychiatry. Both build on the insights of earlier writers from Freud onwards and on their own clinical experience, but draw also upon a great deal of empirical evidence, their own and other people's, which has accrued since Lindemann's time.[17]

It takes a short excursion into psychological bereavement literature to discover that not only do Bowlby and Parkes dominate contemporary thinking on both sides of the Atlantic, but that they have worked so closely at points in the past and feed so frequently on each other's ideas that it is often difficult to see precisely where one writer's thinking ends and the other's begins. This can be illustrated by this comment from the introduction to one of Bowlby's books.

> One to whom I am especially indebted is Colin Murray Parkes. At a time in the early 1960s when I was struggling to clarify the nature of mourning he drew my attention to Darwin's ideas and to the part played by the mourner's urge to recover the lost person. Subsequently we joined forces and he began his studies of widows, first in London and later in Boston, which have made such a big contribution to our understanding. He has read through the chapters in Part II of this volume on the mourning of adults and has made a large number of valuable criticisms and suggestions.[18]

We can talk about the Bowlby-Parkes approach to bereavement study as one to which practically all contemporary theorists would subscribe. It will be mainly to their writings or to those of their adherents that I shall be referring in describing the contemporary understanding of the grief process.

The major works of both are well known. Parkes' most famous book is *Bereavement: Studies of Grief in Adult Life*.[19] Bowlby is best known for his massive three-volume work *Attachment and Loss*.[20] The starting point for this is not bereavement but the mechanics of attachment behaviour between parents and children, the process of the formation of human relationships and early experiences of separation. Bereavement is thus eventually seen in a much broader context of human experience. This approach has come to be called *Attachment Theory*. Bereavement is the irreversible disruption of an attachment bond. The advantage of this approach as a framework for bereavement study has been summed up in the following words:

> By conceptualising the grief process as a form of separation anxiety, attachment theory offers a plausible theoretical interpretation of many aspects of normal and pathological grieving which have not been explained by other theories. Thus attachment theory can explain paradoxical symptoms of grief like the urge to

search for the lost person, the feeling of the presence of the deceased, or anger about having been deserted. It also allows one to identify antecedents of different forms of pathological grief. Finally it can offer an explanation for the cross-cultural invariance of the core symptoms of grief.[21]

This is the dominant theoretical concept underlying the study of grief and bereavement today.

The Stages of Grief

Both Bowlby and Parkes describe the process of grieving as consisting of four stages, which Bowlby calls: (1) Numbing (2) Yearning and searching (3) Disorganisation (4) Reorganisation.[22] This sequence is followed by other writers.[23] Sometimes these stages are expanded by isolating individual features, thus making longer lists.[24] In the rest of this chapter, I shall describe these stages, focusing particularly on some of the striking features of the second stage of 'searching' in the Bowlby-Parkes model.

Numbing

For many bereaved people, the first emotion on encountering or hearing about the death of a loved one is one of numbness. Parkes' original research, on which his book *Bereavement* is based, involved a sample of young widows in London. He describes how many of them felt a sense of numbness or 'blunting'. This began in the first few minutes and continued for no more than a few hours or days.[25] This seems to be typical of the experience of bereaved people. Another writer in the tradition of Parkes and Bowlby, Beverly Raphael, gives a vivid description of this early phase.

> The first response to the news of the death of a loved one is one of shock, numbness and disbelief. The bereaved feels a sense of unreality, as though what has been said or what has happened could not possibly be true — as though it could not have been said, as though it must be happening to someone else.[26]

She depicts this experience as a sort of denial of what is happening and this is probably an accurate interpretation. It is, however, for most people, a temporary denial because, at least in the case of a normal grief, it is a denial struggling with the insistent demands of reality. Also, in the normal course of grief, it is reality which will, slowly and painfully, assert itself at centre stage. This is why, except in pathological cases, this phase is short-lived.

A number of things will in time force the acceptance of reality onto the consciousness of the bereaved person: the need to inform other people of the death; the sorting out of legal or insurance details; the making of arrangements for the funeral; possibly the viewing of the body and, most importantly, the funeral service itself. Raphael speaks of 'a progressive intrusion of the reality of the absence of the dead person which leads to a lessening of denial.'[27]

Many bereaved people describe this emergence from numbness as the clearing of a mist or the gradual wearing off of an anaesthetic, making the sufferer vulnerable to the full onset of emotional pain. It is at this point that the human consciousness begins to adjust to the hard fact of loss. It is to what follows that people are usually referring when they speak of grief.

Yearning and Searching

Typically the bereaved person moves from a state of numbness to one of intense and painful awareness. 'In humans,' says Parkes, 'there are indications from many sources that the grieving person is in a state of high arousal during much of the time and this occasionally approaches pain.' During this period, 'the most characteristic feature of grief is not prolonged depression but acute and episodic pangs . . . Bowlby has called this the phase of yearning and pining.'[28]

But what precisely is going on during this period of pining? One of the most significant contributions of the partnership of Parkes and Bowlby to the study of bereavement has been their attribution of this feature of grief to the mechanisms of searching. Both seem to have arrived at this conclusion from separate starting points but to have considerably influenced each other en route.

For Bowlby the idea did not originate directly from the study of bereavement but from his observations of children separated from their parents in hospital. It may well have been Bowlby's research which, in the last couple of decades, has been the principal influence in the change of policy in British hospitals with respect to the access of parents to their children. He describes this research in the second volume of his *magnum opus*, called *Separation*, but the comparison between the distress of such children and the experience of adult bereavement seems to permeate all of his thinking in this area.

Parkes' starting point, on the other hand, is the biological function of animal behaviour and he makes frequent comparisons between humans and other species. For instance:

> Pining is the subjective and emotional component of the urge to search for a lost object. I maintain that an adult human being has the same impulse to search that is shown among many species of social animals.[29]

The concept is that humans (and other social animals) experience countless instances of separation from loved ones, the vast majority of a temporary nature. Searching mechanisms are set into action automatically and these are *almost* invariably rewarded by the finding of the lost loved one. Separation by death is such a relatively rare occurrence in one lifetime that mind and body instinctively set into motion the searching processes. In this case, however, the efforts are doomed to frustration. In Bowlby's words:

> Irretrievable loss is statistically so unusual that it is not taken into account . . . all losses are assumed to be retrievable and are responded to accordingly.[30]

The acute anxiety of this stage is thus related to the urge to search that we feel whenever someone we care for is inexplicably missing. This sensation is all the more urgent when the missing person is someone for whose safety we have felt responsible. It occurs amongst herds of wild animals as well as in human society. Humans will often find ingenious expressions of this instinct to search despite the conscious awareness that death has taken place. Parkes instances the appeal of spiritualism, as one avenue for the searching impulse.[31] The hypothesis of grief as searching has proved very fruitful. Not only does it explain the acute sense of distress encountered at this stage, but it also gives an intelligible framework for understanding some specific experiences of bereavement that have sometimes been described as distinct 'phases'. Among these are the experiences of hallucination and anger.

Hallucination

Because the work of searching is so exhausting and so painful, many bereaved people find temporary relief in an imagined presence of the dead loved one. This in itself is not connected to any pathological development. Provided that such pretence is not clung to tenaciously and does not become a permanent feature of the consciousness of the bereaved person, it can provide a kind of short-term relief from pain which can be used for the regathering of strength to continue with the tasks of grieving. Parkes says about one group of widows he surveyed: 'Often the widow's progress towards recovery was facilitated by inner conversations with her husband's presence . . . this continued sense of attachment was not incompatible with increasing capacity for independent action.'[32]

For many bereaved people the sense that their loved one is near is more than a deliberately imagined presence. The phenomenon of hallucinatory appearances of the deceased is quite common. Such an occurrence is explicable in terms of the *searching* hypothesis of attachment theory. This will be understandable to anyone who has had the experience of searching for a familiar face in a crowd — a friend who has not turned up at an arranged meeting place or a child who has wandered off. A common experience is that of 'seeing' the person's likeness sometimes in people who bear very little physical resemblance. What is happening in these cases is simple. A mental image of the lost person is formed and the searcher scans the environment for a *match*. When this is not found it can sometimes be invented by the distressed mind.

In the case of bereavement, 'matches' may be found in all kinds of unexpected ways and, far from always being a consciously chosen method of mitigating pain, they may arrive in forms totally uncalled for. Such images may be visual — the sight of someone in their favourite chair or glimpsed in the mirror — or audial — the sound of someone coming through the door at their normal homecoming time or a voice heard clearly in the state between sleeping and waking.

One survey conducted in Wales revealed that almost half of the 293 people interviewed had postbereavement hallucinations. These hallucinations often occurred over a period of many years and at the time of interview over a third of the subjects were still experiencing them. The researcher found no variation of cultural or religious background to account for this phenomenon and concluded not only that 'hallucinations are normal experiences after widowhood' but also that their effect is in general helpful.[33] If such experiences are really so common then it is extremely important that people are aware of them and see them for what they are: a perfectly normal and explicable psychological phenomenon and not a precursor of madness or evidence of 'psychic' phenomena vulnerable to exploitation by those with spiritualistic leanings.

Anger

Another aspect of grief which can cause great distress to bereaved people and those close to them is the heightened sense of anger and aggression which is often experienced. One writer instances as typical the widow who gave her doctor 'a good hiding'. He comments, 'It was as if her rage, while it lasted, had given her courage.'[34] This feature also is given a plausible rationale within attachment theory and the hypothesis of searching. The idea is that the aggression accompanying searching has a specific 'biological' function. Anger is expressed towards the lost one to discourage him from wandering off again. Thus the young animal who wanders from the herd will often be 'punished' by its parent — as is the young child who gets lost in the supermarket! The usefulness of this is evident. For animals in the wild, as for very young humans, separation often means danger. The anger is thus a concomitant of love. It is easy to see now the irrelevance of the scholarly debate over whether grief or anger is to be seen as the dominant emotion of Jesus at the tomb of Lazarus!

Bowlby explains this feature in bereavement in terms of the relative rarity of irretrievable loss.[35] Anger in the case of bereavement thus only appears irrational. Its primary focus, it seems, is on the lost loved one despite the obvious facts that not only is the deceased (in most cases) not to blame for dying, but also that no amount of scolding can bring him back and encourage him not to leave again. Thus the bereaved's mental processes are in conflict with her instinctive behaviour. As Raphael says:

> The bereaved does indeed know intellectually, cognitively, that the lost one will not return; yet the whole assumptive world is still orientated toward him and has not yet realigned to a new set of configurations and assumptions . . . (hence) anger and aggression are common.[36]

Anger in bereavement then is an explicable phenomenon. In many cases, of course, it is impossible for the bereaved to admit that it is the lost loved one with whom she feels angry. The anger is thus displaced onto a convenient third party. This may well be someone connected in the bereaved's mind with the death. Hence the fate of the poor doctor mentioned above. Indeed the medical and nursing professions are frequently the objects of such 'irrational' rage. In other cases it could well be a member of the clergy, a bereavement counsellor, a relative or friend — or perhaps God himself.

Whether or not a would-be helper becomes the target of anger could well depend upon the stance he is perceived as taking in relation to the death. Resentment is likely to focus upon anyone seen as impeding the search or making it less likely to end in satisfaction — anyone that is who, as Bowlby says, at this stage counsels acceptance.[37]

It is evident then that, on this understanding, anger is not to be seen as a separate 'stage' of bereavement which is encountered, passed through and overcome in one episode. It is rather one feature of the process of searching which will alternate with periods of deep distress, intense pining and even brief times of mitigation and an imagined sense of presence. No wonder therefore that for the bereaved person in this phase the world often seems to have lost all predictability and meaning. Parkes sums up:

> But the world of the bereaved is in chaos. Because they are striving to find what cannot be found they ignore what can be found. They feel as if the most central, important aspect of themselves is gone and all that is left is meaningless and irrelevant — hence the world itself has become meaningless and irrelevant.[38]

Disorganisation

This distressing period is only brought to an end as repeated frustrations bring home the reality that the search is in vain. Bowlby again:

> For mourning to have a favourable outcome it appears to be necessary for a bereaved person to endure this buffeting of emotion. Only if he can tolerate the pining, the more or less conscious searching, the seemingly endless examination of how and why the loss occurred, the anger at anyone who might be responsible, not sparing even the dead person, can he come gradually to recognize and accept that the loss is in truth permanent and that his life must be shaped anew.[39]

Raphael describes how this process operates in personal experience:

> Each time the bereaved holds the image of the deceased and looks for the familiar interactions to turn it into reality, and this does not occur, the reality and the finality of the loss are re-inforced. Thus this yearning, longing and pining for the lost person are part of the adaptation to the loss, part of the reality testing that must slowly and painfully occur as his absence continues.[40]

The ending of the phase of searching, however, is not the end of the grieving process. Much less is it what we might call 'relief'. It begins what Raphael calls a stage of review in which the relationship and its loss are assessed. She goes on to list the common emotions associated with this process of review as sadness, regret, guilt, relief, and despair. It is easy to see why this third phase has been described as that of 'disorganisation' and 'despair'. The feeling of sadness seems to characterize this period.

Raphael insists on the importance of accepting *sadness* as a normal and necessary part of this stage of grief and of not confusing it with the medical term *depression*. For example:

> There is often a semantic confusion: many bereaved people identify their sadness as 'depression', for the word 'sad' seems infrequently used and little recognized in the language of much contemporary Western society. Sad or depressed feelings when labelled 'depression' may lead a person to receive treatment for an illness, depression, when he may actually be experiencing only the sadness that accompanies the normal bereavement process.[41]

At this stage also we see the bereaved person suffering emotions from which she might well want to escape. In the previous phase there was the sense of yearning and pining; this is now followed by a feeling of intense sadness as the reality of loss is accepted. One common strategy of avoidance might be, as Raphael says, to seek refuge in medical treatment for depression. Other means which are often used include alcohol, social activity, enforced jollity, work and — most seductively for some — the comforts of religion. In all these cases what is happening once more is an avoidance of reality, not at this stage the reality of loss but of the real emotional state of the bereaved person. But it is only by enduring sadness that she can move on to the next stage.

Reorganisation

If all goes well, the bereaved person will emerge from these phases and gradually be able to take up life again with interest and genuine engagement. Parkes refers to this final stage of the grieving process as finding a *new identity*. At first this phrase may seem something of an overstatement. Could we not really be speaking of the resumption of a restored old identity? Parkes looks at this in the context of the ever-changing process of life. He states the fascinating hypothesis that 'it would seem that the experience of bereavement may throw light on some fundamental questions concerning the nature of identity.' He goes on:

> My body is constantly changing. Old cells die and new ones are born to replace them. Only a minority of the living beings which make up my multicellular organism were alive five years ago. Within my brain the changes are more slow. As I grow older nerve cells die but none replaces them. The part of me that perceives, directs and remembers is gradually dwindling. Age is carrying out a series of minute lobotomy operations on me, and my personality is slowly being altered. Fortunately the change is gradual and it is possible for me to maintain the illusion that I am the person I thought I was 5 years ago. Unless, that is, something occurs which suddenly proves to me that I am not.[42]

A bereavement is, according to Parkes, just such an experience. It shatters the illusion that we are still the same by forcing upon us a new identity within a new pattern of relationship with the world. We have seen that the process leading to the acceptance of the changed pattern is long, hard and painful. The changes in life-style transcend the trivial details that are immediately apparent:

> A major change in life, such as that produced by the death of a spouse, not only alters expectations at the level of the focal action patterns (How many teaspoons to lay on the breakfast table?) but also the overall plans and roles of which these form a part. A widow is no longer a wife; she is a widow.[43]

If Parkes is correct in saying that it is not sufficient to resume an old identity as the outcome of bereavement but rather that it is necessary to find a new one, the question must inevitably arise as to what will determine the shape of the eventual identity which will be taken up? Parkes has a surprising answer to this question. In a book co-written with Robert Weiss, he states:

> To a marked degree religious and cultural views about death define what it is that the bereaved will have to accept.[44]

The same writers then go on to indicate what kind of religious or cultural views will offer a basic minimum of support to the bereaved in forming this new identity:

> It is necessary . . . that there be recognition that loss has occurred and acceptance of being currently without a partner. These are inescapable realities that must be integrated into the widow or widower's current identity.[45]

Thus, as we come to the end of a survey of the secular, psychological theory of the process of bereavement, we find one of its principal spokespersons pleading for a cultural or religious orientation which will support the bereaved in finding a new identity without the loved one by enabling them to accept the realities of loss. In fact, the acceptance of reality has been an implicit theme throughout the whole description of the grieving process. In the next chapter we shall see just how vital this acceptance is and how important it is for the grieving person to have a religious orientation which encourages the acceptance and not the denial of reality.

Chapter 9

HOW DOES GRIEF GO WRONG?

Psychologists like Colin Murray Parkes and John Bowlby who have studied bereavement in considerable detail have encouraged us to see grief as a process. It is hard work for those involved in it and always extremely painful, but, rather like the healing of severed skin or a broken bone, provided that the circumstances are right, there is a natural succession of stages which will in most cases result in a satisfactory outcome. This does not mean, of course, that the lost loved one will be forgotten but that a resolution of conflicting feelings will have taken place allowing the bereaved person to resume their life with a new sense of identity and be ready, where appropriate, to establish new relationships.

Anyone who has encountered more than a handful of grieving people, however, will know that life is not always so simple. Some people do not flow through the phases of grief to a good outcome — even allowing for the fluctuations between phases which Parkes teaches us to expect. In some cases a particular phase seems to continue interminably, even after many years — or may never seem to be reached. The prospect of a satisfactory ending to painful grief might seem an impossible goal. It might even be a prospect firmly resisted by the bereaved person.

For some unfortunates the course of grief might lead to a breakdown or to the eventual diagnosis of some clinical mental illness. It should be remembered that the origins of the study of the psychological process of grief lie in the world of clinical psychiatry. Parkes once described grief itself as a 'functional psychiatric disorder' but added that it is one 'whose cause is known, whose features are distinctive and whose course is predictable.'[1] Grief is a kind of psychiatric disturbance which, for the most part, contains within itself the seeds of its own healing. There are occasions, however, when the natural course of healing does not take place.

For every disturbed bereaved person who finds themself receiving psychiatric treatment of one kind or another, there are scores more who simply go about their daily lives suffering the apparently endless symptoms of a grief which has gone wrong. It is a phenomenon familiar to doctors, counsellors and ministers and perhaps, like me, many have found that it is not at all uncommon among professing Christians.

So, an important question to ask is: What causes grief to go wrong, resulting in a state which the psychologists would refer to as pathological? One interesting feature which has emerged from our survey of the psychological literature is that pathological or disturbed grief is not a different kind of grief. It occurs not when grief follows a *different* course from normal but when it encounters a disturbance *within* its course. It results when a feature of the normal process is frustrated or exaggerated. It was E. Lindemann who first drew attention to this in his study of the relatives of those who died in the 'Cocoanut Grove' fire and it has become a commonplace in bereavement study. John Bowlby, for instance, writes:

> The more detailed the picture we obtain of healthy mourning the more clearly we are able to identify the pathological variants as being the result of defensive processes having interfered with and diverted its course.[2]

I shall return to these 'defensive processes' later. For now I simply note that it is a disturbance in the normal process which causes the problems.

Types of Pathological Grief

Bowlby and Parkes are, as usual, unanimous in their analysis of the major types of pathological grief although they employ different terms. There are two. The first Parkes calls *delayed*[3] and Bowlby *prolonged absence of conscious*[4] grieving. The effect is the same. The person concerned has lost a loved one. However for a prolonged period the loss seems unreal. Even after a long time the person 'cannot take it in'. He or she is unable to cry. The expected sense of pain and yearning does not come.

Although this may superficially appear as a relief, for such individuals and those close to them the effects can be bewildering and distressing. They appear to themselves and others as 'unnatural'. On the other hand such a person could be described as 'taking it well' when in fact something is very much amiss. Someone who in this way seemed to 'cope well' may months later be suddenly and inexplicably overtaken by acute and painful grief.

The second variant is called by Parkes *prolonged* and by Bowlby *chronic* grief. In this case the symptoms of grief are all too evident. The problem is that after a long time the symptoms have not abated. The acute pangs of grief or the dull sadness of acknowledged loss seem endless. This can last for many years and sometimes, particularly in the case of elderly people, for the rest of life.

It can be seen at once that these phenomena can be related to the four phases of grief which we saw in the last chapter. Bowlby says:

> Absence of conscious grieving can be regarded as a pathologically prolonged extension of the phase of numbing, whereas the various forms of chronic mourning can be regarded as extended or distorted versions of the phases of yearning and searching [or of] disorganisation and despair.[5]

The major forms of disturbed grief therefore are seen by psychologists as blockages in the natural flow of grieving which would, if left unhindered, carry the bereaved person through the painful process leading eventually to resolution and healing. This insight is of great importance in terms of the Christian understanding of bereavement. It seems that a major issue in the process of bereavement is the dilemma of acceptance or denial.

The full acceptance of reality is easier to speak about than to achieve when what is in view is a reality as unpleasant as the death of someone we love. It involves a process which takes time and during this time the human mind will need to defend itself by means of brief periods of mitigation or relief from pain. Such temporary avoidance of reality is perfectly consistent with healthy grief. Parkes, for instance explains how some forms of mitigation 'enable the bereaved person to avoid, consciously or unconsciously, the thoughts that are so painful, or to dissociate the pain from the thoughts.'[6]

In the last chapter we noted how, in the acute phase of pining, some bereaved people find relief in the pretence that the lost loved one is still around and how sometimes the unconscious mind seeks relief in spontaneous hallucinations. Such defensive techniques are not in themselves harmful, and can even be helpful when used to provide a breathing space in a learning process aimed in the direction of honesty and the acceptance of reality. When this is happening there will be a continuous oscillation between avoidance and acceptance with the acceptance of reality gradually gaining the upper hand. The consensus among the psychological authorities on bereavement is that it is the alternation between avoidance and acceptance, distancing and confrontation with the truth, which produces a healthy outcome.[7]

The bereaved often find themselves, therefore, torn between a conservative and a progressive impulse, a backward and a forward pull. When the general movement is forwards, all is well, but when the backward forces gain the upper hand and progress is halted or reversed, then the bereaved person is in difficulty. In this case necessary and healthy avoidance has become dangerous denial.[8] This struggle between acceptance and denial is not over in one battle. The reality to be accepted changes as the bereaved move through the phases of grief. At each stage a fresh battle has to be fought and won.

In order to emerge healthily from each phase of the grieving process, there is demanded of the bereaved the acceptance of a particular aspect of reality. It is the struggle between the acceptance and denial of this reality which makes grieving so difficult. The continuous overcoming of denial and the acknowledgement of reality both consciously and unconsciously at each point can be said to be the *work* of grieving.

The Work of Grieving

At the *numbness* phase, it will be remembered, the bereaved person is in a state of shock. The conscious mind may have accepted that the loved one is dead but the unconscious is not prepared to accept this truth so readily. The person therefore feels numb or distant from reality. He or she is saying, 'I can't believe that it's true.' In order to move on from this phase the truth to be accepted is that

death has taken place.

Normally this reality will force itself upon the mind within a matter of hours or days. The mist will clear, painful reality will emerge and the next phase will begin. When this does not happen, when denial proves stronger than acceptance, then there ensues a state of delayed or prolonged absence of grieving.

At the phase of *searching and pining* the person is engaged in a more or less unconscious search for the lost loved one. Mental processes are set in motion which are working towards finding someone who is temporarily missing. The mind scans the world for a match, sometimes resulting in hallucinations. It generates anger at the deserter which easily gets displaced onto other people. Only continued frustration in this hopeless search eventually convinces the individual that their loved one will not be found. The aspect of reality to be accepted at this stage is that

death is permanent.

If this reality is not fully taken in, the person will find themself locked in a chronic state of anxiety and restlessness.

At the phase where loss is accepted, referred to by some as the phase of *disorganisation and despair*, the bereaved person battles with feelings of intense sadness, loss and loneliness. It may be that these feelings come at a point in time when those around or even the sufferer themself, feel that they should be 'over it'. For this phase to be resolved the pain must be experienced. It is at this point that the bereaved might be most tempted to attempt to force themselves into a state of normality or jollity or to take refuge in antidepressant medication. The reality to be accepted here is that of

the experience of feelings of loss.

When the reality of these feelings is denied, a different form of chronic grief may set in despite all attempts to overcome it: a lingering sadness which might be confused with, or may even result in, clinical depression.

The final phase is one where, loss having been come to terms with, a *new identity* must be formed. The sufferer may not want to accept this new identity. He or she may now acknowledge that their loss is real but may want to cling to vestiges of the life lived when a now departed relationship was alive. Or they may even wish to return to the lost identity they held before their now dead loved one was a part of their life. In order to move on from this point the reality to be accepted is that they are now living in

a new situation.

If this reality is denied the bereaved may appear to have recovered from the major symptoms of grief but may still be living a life locked in the past and perhaps finding great difficulty in forming new relationships.

Faith and the Work of Grieving

It is in this struggle between the acceptance and denial of successive aspects of reality that strongly held religious views can have a positive or negative effect upon the grieving process. Christian faith in particular can play a crucial role in facilitating or frustrating a healthy outcome from grief. It is interesting to note that the leading psychologists of bereavement, while not antagonistic to the place of faith in recovery from bereavement, nonetheless seem to hold an ambivalent attitude towards it. One important survey of depression in widowhood found an association between what the researchers call 'religiosity' and good outcome from bereavement. Of a group of depressed widows it was found that 50% never attended church while this figure was only 17% in a non-depressed group.[9] Another survey found that 59% of widows thought that religion had been a great source of comfort to them during their bereavement.[10]

Nevertheless it is clear that there is a generally held belief that religious faith can work two ways. Parkes sums up this belief in relation to a survey of young London widows:

> The relationship between religion and adjustment . . . is not simple. There was some evidence that those whose religious beliefs helped them to place the bereavement in a meaningful perspective coped better with bereavement than those who had no such faith, but it was also true that several of the regular

church-attenders did not make out well. The view of God as a protecting, loving father was hard to maintain in the face of untimely bereavement, and the possibility of reunion in days to come did not help the widow to tolerate the absence of her husband now.[11]

It seems to me that Parkes is making a number of points in this statement which are relevant to the theme of this book:

(1) Religious faith can be seen as contributing to good or bad outcomes;
(2) Faith is most helpful when it provides a perspective in which bereavement can be understood;
(3) Perhaps surprisingly, belief in life after death is not such a comfort as might have been expected.

What the psychologists do not do, of course, is grapple with the question of what it is about Christian faith which makes the difference between helpfulness and unhelpfulness. The key to this, I have come to believe, lies precisely in the conflict between the acceptance or denial of reality at each phase of the grieving process.

Let us take the *numbness* phase first. At this early stage, as we have seen, the bereaved person struggles with the acceptance or denial that death has taken place. If the person is a Christian — or if they are being helped, comforted or counselled by someone with a strong Christian ethos — the voice of faith may be saying to them one of two things at this point. One kind of Christianity may readily collude with denial. *Death is an illusion. The Christian does not really die. Your loved one has simply passed into a different realm*. This language may even be used in the funeral service. In how many such services, for example have the familiar words of Henry Scott Holland been read?

> Death is nothing at all . . . I have only slipped away into the next room . . . It is the same as it ever was; there is absolute unbroken continuity . . . I am waiting for you for an interval, somewhere very near, just around the corner. All is well.[12]

On the other hand, a different kind of faith might speak with a different voice. It might affirm that, whatever may occur in the future, death is a reality. It might reflect the perspective of Jesus for whom, unlike Socrates, death was a cup he would rather pass from him or the language of Paul for whom death was not 'nothing at all' but 'the last enemy'. It will be evident here that whether faith denies or accepts the reality that death has taken place will make a difference as to whether or not it will be a helpful resource to the bereaved.

Similarly, during the phase of *searching and pining*, there may be two voices of faith. Here the battle is for the acceptance that separation is permanent. But is that so for the Christian? One kind of faith might, with apparent validity, say, *This is only for a little while. Soon you will be reunited 'on the other shore'*. Indeed, this is such a commonplace of Christian comfort for the bereaved that many Christians may be shocked to hear its helpfulness questioned.

The objection to it is not just that, from a psychological perspective, it could keep a believer locked in a phase of anxious pining, unable to accept the fullness of loss, but also that, from a theological perspective, it has no biblical basis as a comfort for bereavement. Clearly the Christian expects life beyond this one and there seems no good reason to deny that we shall be recognisable to each other. However there is an alternative Christian approach that takes seriously the fact that within this life, where grief is experienced, there is no hope of regaining contact, despite the spiritualists' claims. This approach might also take on board, particularly in the case of widowhood, the argument of Jesus that relationships in the next life are of a different order. The point here would be that the relationship, if not the person, is truly and permanently lost. There is something here to grieve for and a loss to be fully accepted.

At the stage of *acceptance of loss* the central problem is to cope with unpleasant feelings of sadness. Again we might find Christian faith speaking with two different voices. Just as some seek relief from this kind of experience through antidepressant drugs, others through the abuse of alcohol and still others by forcing themselves into a social whirl where a superficial happiness is expected and enforced, many Christians find refuge in the 'promises' of faith. *After all, the Christian life is meant to be characterized by joy. The Christian should know victory in Christ over negative emotions. 'The joy of the Lord is your strength.'*

Unfortunately, for such feelings as sadness to be overcome, they have first to be acknowledged and experienced freely. We have seen how biblical characters undergoing bereavement gave full vent to their emotion. There may equally therefore be a voice of faith which allows the Christian to find comfort in suffering not through denial but, like Paul (e.g. in Philippians 3:10), in subsuming their personal suffering to the sufferings of Christ; acknowledging that the pain of Good Friday and the silence of Saturday have to be accepted and lived through in order to arrive at the elation of Easter Sunday.

During the final phase the bereaved person is often struggling to come to terms with a new situation in which he or she is compelled to take on a *new identity*. This can be a very threatening experience because it involves the acceptance of change. Here too a person's view of the nature of Christianity is crucial and one of two approaches may be adopted. A person's Christian faith may identify with the conservative impulse in us all, the aspect of our personality which constantly pulls us back towards the safety of what has always been. For some this represents the very essence of Christianity: it is that which offers us immutability in a constantly changing world. Such Christians will love singing the hymn which contains the lines:

> And safe is such confiding
> For nothing changes here.[13]

On the other hand a bereaved person's Christian faith may identify with the forward movement which pushes us onwards. Such a person sees the life of faith as a pilgrimage or growth. This attitude again identifies with Paul who saw the progress of faith as being 'transformed into the same image from one degree of glory to another' (2 Corinthians 3:18). Despite the inevitable pain of leaving the past behind, it will more readily discern hope in the future as the sufferer emerges from grief. As we have seen in the last chapter, oscillation between forward and backward movement is characteristic of the whole grieving process. At this stage the progressive element is vital in propelling the bereaved into the flow of life.

What emerges from this discussion is a model which combines the phases of grief and the tasks of grieving in each stage drawn from psychological bereavement literature with alternative 'voices' emerging from Christian tradition. It can be set out as follows:

NUMBNESS
Acceptance or denial that death has taken place

(a) *Death is unreal for the Christian.*
(b) *Death is the 'last enemy' which has to be faced.*

SEARCHING AND PINING
Acceptance or denial that death is permanent

(a) *One day soon we shall meet again.*
(b) *We shall never again share what we had in this life.*

ACCEPTANCE OF LOSS
Acceptance or denial of feelings of sadness

(a) *The Christian life should always be full of joy.*
(b) *The Christian should expect to share Christ's suffering in the hope of sharing also his resurrection.*

NEW IDENTITY
Acceptance of a new situation

(a) *The Christian life offers unchanging reality.*
(b) *The Christian life is one of ongoing spiritual growth.*

Healthy Grieving

The question inevitably arises as to what kind of Christianity is likely to encourage responses which collude with denial in the grieving process and what kind will encourage the acceptance at each phase which will allow the grieving person to complete the appropriate tasks and move on. If we were to group together the responses labelled (a) in the model above and then those labelled (b), it is obvious that the distinct outlooks they represent would transcend any denominational boundaries. A Baptist, for example, is not likely to be more prone to denial or to acceptance of reality than an Anglican! Nor would the distinction we are concerned with here fit neatly into any schemes of churchmanship. Evangelicals, Catholics or liberals are as likely to find themselves in either camp.

What we are concerned with here are attitudes stemming from distinctive orientations to death and the afterlife. We have seen from the historical examples cited that, in its origins in the pagan world and its most authoritative expression in Christianity, the 'immortalist' or what we have called the 'Platonic-Augustinian' orientation has, first of all, tended to minimize death. For the Platonic philosopher or for the Augustinian Christian death is an illusion, not to be taken seriously. Where physical death occurs, the logic of a belief in immortality is that the separation which it causes is of a temporary nature. We have seen that this belief is classically accompanied by a most strenuous suppression of the emotions associated with grieving. It can be argued, moreover, that immortalists are, like Augustine, more likely to despise the body and to see this life as the anteroom of the next, which is often expected to be one of rather static contemplation.

The doctrine of resurrection, on the other hand, stems uniquely from the Judaeo-Christian tradition enshrined in the Bible and the intertestamental Jewish writings. Because, in its Christian form, its supreme model is the death and resurrection of Jesus, it is able, while offering a positive hope for the transcendence of death, to allow death its full horror and loss. Because it promises resurrection to a life of a different order, it affirms the temporary nature of relationships in this life and thus a sense of the permanence of loss. For these reasons it casts no shadow of suppression on the flow of the emotions of grief and both Old Testament Israelites and New Testament Christians (following the example of Christ himself) exhibit the full range of such feelings. Because it points to a resurrection of full person-hood, including the body, it confers a dignity on this bodily life also and encourages respect for human growth and development.

During all four phases of the grieving process, therefore, this distinction can be shown to have a striking relevance. The outstanding features of these orientations, moreover, will be shown in later chapters to be as much in evidence in the contemporary Christian experience of bereavement as in the ancient texts.

A proviso must be added at this point. It is not being claimed, nor can it be, that a belief in the natural immortality of the soul is a certain predictor of a pathological outcome of bereavement! This is so for at least two reasons. First, most modern Christians have very little idea of the nature of their view of life after death.

Many would give a description of what they believe containing elements of both, or would assert different claims at different times and in different contexts. What is certain, however, is that both the tendency towards denial and the tendency towards the acceptance of reality and the successful resolution of grief are current among Christians of all kinds today. My contention is that the element of denial is much more common than it ought to be, and creates havoc in the bereavement process of many Christians whose faith ought to be a resource and not a complicating factor in their grief. I believe that where this occurs its origin can be traced to what I have called the 'Platonic-Augustinian' attitude to death and grief.

Moreover, there are many other determining factors of the outcome of grief beside one's view of the afterlife. Beverly Raphael lists six such factors. They are:

(1) The pre-existing relationship between the bereaved and the deceased.
(2) The type of death — sudden or anticipated.
(3) The response of the family and the social network.
(4) Other concurrent stress or crises.
(5) Previous losses.
(6) Sociodemographic factors.[14]

The relationship of some of these factors to pathological outcomes are well documented. Sudden, unanticipated death is known to be related to delayed grief while an ambivalent or overdependent relationship before death can often lead to chronic grief. Family and friends of the bereaved can play a large part in encouraging or suppressing the expression of feelings.

Raphael does not even mention religious belief as a predictive factor, probably because of the conflicting nature of the evidence already alluded to. What I am saying here, however, is perfectly in line with the statement of Parkes and Weiss that any form of denial requires that 'continued attention be given to maintaining a belief system contrary to reality.'[15] Such a belief system is likely to create a predisposition to a complicated grief particularly when combined with one of the factors listed by Raphael. A believer may in fact be emotionally and psychologically more healthy than his belief system, but the effect of that system cannot be ignored as an element in the process of grief.

Chapter 10

HOW TO HELP THE GRIEVING

This book is not meant to be a manual on bereavement counselling. It has set out to answer a *why* rather than a *how* question. Nevertheless, it might be helpful at this point to draw out some practical implications from what we have learned so far in this enquiry and to address briefly the question of what it is that the bereaved really need.

The first thing to say is that the bereaved need to know that their grief is valid in the midst of a culture which denies both the fact of death and the pain of grieving. In chapter seven, we explored ways in which our society conspires to deny the fact of death. It is interesting therefore to note how those who have studied the experience of the bereaved from a psychological perspective have found the suffering of their subjects denied or minimized. One group of researchers reported

> our convincing documentation of the objective importance of insensitivity, overt or covert hostility, absence of empathy, and ignorance of a widow's needs — all of which recur in the statements made to widows by significant others. For there is abundant evidence that the behaviour of many people in the environment of the recently bereaved widow, including some members of the so-called 'helping professions', is in active opposition to those psychological processes required for the satisfactory resolution of object loss.[1]

Although written some years ago, those words sum up the experience of many bereaved people in our society today. It has been demonstrated, moreover, that those who find that their social network discourages the expression of the emotions of grief are more likely to experience a pathological outcome to their bereavement.[2]

It sometimes seems that, despite the universality of the grief experience, we in our Western civilisation are involved in a social conspiracy to hide and inhibit grief with potentially disastrous results for many people. The following passage describes what often goes on:

> We look at others around us, see people steeling themselves against grief, denying it, wallowing in it, avoiding open discussion and 'protecting' those who are younger and weaker. And this melange of human expression is the more confusing because some of it does not ring true. Honesty is put aside and the dead or dying person is spoken of in an incomplete way.[3]

It can no longer be assumed that bereaved people will find the acceptance of their situation that they need in their normal social environment. Those who seek to provide a context in which the bereaved can speak freely of their experiences will not only be meeting an urgent need in our society but contributing to a counter-culture for the sake of the grieving.

Parkes laments the absence of any public recognition of grief in our society. He describes a typical group of younger widows in one of his surveys as . . . 'a group of unstable young women, unprepared for bereavement, members of a society, and within that society of a generation, which has largely abandoned both the formal expression of mourning and belief in the efficacy of ritual'. He concludes with the following indictment upon our society in this area where, he believes, the bereaved have been failed so badly: 'the absence today of social expectations and rituals facilitating mourning is likely to contribute to the occurrence of pathological reactions to bereavement.'[4]

The first and most desperate need of the bereaved therefore is permission for their grief and the creation of some kind of space and opportunity in which to express it.

Support

Since the very beginning of the psychological study of bereavement the process of grief has been referred to as a kind of 'work'. The grieving have a job to do; they have tasks to perform. The stages of grief isolated by Bowlby, Parkes and others are really a way of analysing the work — breaking down the job into manageable units. The next important thing for a would-be helper to realize is that these are tasks that only the grieving themselves can accomplish.

What then can be the function of someone who wants to help in the situation? At its most basic it is to be there and to be attentive. There is no doubt that the consensus of opinion is that the best help that the bereaved can receive is to be supported through the grieving process. They should be firmly but gently encouraged to do the work of grieving. This process has its own pace. It must not be impeded, nor should it be rushed.

> The helper should not 'pluck at the heart strings' of the bereaved person until breakdown occurs any more than he or she should connive with the bereaved in endless attempts to avoid the grief work. Both probing and 'jollying along' are unhelpful. The bereaved person has a painful and difficult task to perform which cannot be avoided and cannot be rushed. True help consists in recognising this fact and in helping the bereaved person to arrange things in whatever way is necessary to set him or her free for the task of grieving.[5]

What the bereaved need more than anything else from their helpers is the rare skill of attentive listening. It may be, of course, that for some more specialized help is needed, for example when a blockage is so severe that it results in mental distress or breakdown. Nevertheless even when this occurs, the work of the professional is more demanding in skill but not different in function from that of the listening friend:

> His or her highly skilled tasks will be, among others, the promotion of mourning where this has been suppressed, assistance in dealing with denial when this is gross, protracted and dysfunctional, support in reviewing the lost relationship, promotion of free discussion about the widow's events and interactions within her social network, and possibly some re-examination of earlier losses which may be important factors in hindering her current expression of grief, rage and self-reproach.[6]

So the helping function even of the professional is not to direct grief onto a different course but to allow the normal process to continue or restart after a hiatus. The aim is to relinquish defences, allowing denial to be overcome so that, once more, the normal process of mourning may continue. It is those who find real listening made available to them in their social network who are least likely to find themselves in the kind of pathology which would make professional help necessary.[7]

Another writer lists the skills which he believes are essential for the bereavement counsellor. All of them relate to this ability to facilitate, encourage and when necessary unblock the grieving process. They are: (1) openness, (2) empathy and catharsis, (3) the encouragement of reminiscences, (4) insistence on and acknowledgement of the loss. He indicates how the would-be helper can easily be guilty of creating blockages or of colluding with the bereaved in her denial of loss or of the experience of grief:

> People often give messages to a bereaved person that it is not appropriate for them to grieve. Some messages are quite direct while others are more subtle. But whether it be a rationalisation that the loss was for the best or a nonresponse on the part of the respondent, the effect is the same. A block is activated, impeding or inhibiting the grief process.[8]

Two principal temptations attend the person who wants to help a grieving friend. One is to inform the grieving of what they should experience in an attempt to move the process along; the other — much more common — is to tell the person what they should not be experiencing, thus inhibiting the expression of the emotional reality of the moment. It is much more difficult to simply be present, accepting the pain of the present moment and yet encouraging a gentle forward movement as this emerges naturally in the process of grief. These two functions, therefore — the sharing of pain and the encouragement of progress — are also things that the bereaved need from their helpers.

Pain-Relief?

'People in pain make us feel helpless' says J. W. Worden.[9] His words were addressed to medical practitioners in the United States and his purpose was to discourage them from a too easy recourse to the use of antidepressant drugs when confronted with bereaved people. He was recognising that when we are faced with someone in emotional pain our instinct is to want to relieve it, to make the pain disappear, to make things better.

Those of us who are not doctors and yet spend time in the company of suffering people do not have access to medication. Nevertheless we have the same temptation to administer pain relief if only verbally. We want to tell the grieving person not to upset himself, that things are not as bad as they appear. The fact is that someone else's emotional pain is very hard to bear. We want to relieve his suffering in order to ease our own. Parkes says of the encounter between a bereaved person and their helper:

> Pain is inevitable in such a case and cannot be avoided. It stems from the awareness of both parties that neither can give the other what they want. The helper cannot bring the person back who is dead and the bereaved person cannot gratify the helper by seeming helped. No wonder that both feel dissatisfied with the encounter.[10]

We have seen that grief is a painful process. If a grieving person does not fully face the pain of each stage, they will not be able to work through it to the next. To control the physical pain of, for example, a cancer sufferer is a worthy and important enterprise. To attempt to relieve the symptoms of emotional pain suffered by the bereaved is potentially disastrous.

> The bereavement resolution will be hampered if those offering support try to block [the process] for instance, by trying to prevent the bereaved from dealing with the reality, by pretending the death has not happened, or by avoiding talking about it. The same will be true if they try to keep the bereaved from acknowledging the absence of the dead person by taking him away from reminders of it, by false assurances that it can be fixed, or by trying to block it out by some other means such as drugs or alcohol.[11]

Those who would like to significantly help a grieving person, therefore, must be prepared for the extremely uncomfortable experience of sharing another's pain without attempting to mitigate it. This may come as a surprise to many who might have understood 'comfort' to be the relief of pain rather than its acceptance.

Encouragement

The sharing of another's pain, important as it is, may seem to be a passive way of helping someone in grief. The best kind of help will include an element of active participation also. We have seen that the resolution of grief involves a progression through a series of stages; also that typically the grieving person will oscillate between forward and backward impulses in her progress through them. Part of the emotional pull will be towards a previous episode of life, when the loved one was still alive and present; there is a desire to return to the past. Also, however, perhaps at first unconsciously, there will be an urge to move onwards towards the eventual goal of establishing a new identity in a new situation in which the loved one, still fondly remembered, is now accepted as being absent.

The bereaved person's helper has the choice of colluding with and encouraging one or other of these impulses. The helper will be on the side of regression every time he encourages the idea that the loved one is not really lost for ever or whenever he discourages the full acceptance of the painful feelings of loss. He will be on the side of progress whenever he encourages the appropriate forward dynamic at each stage of the process. What this means in practice will be obvious from the analysis of the stages of bereavement in the previous two chapters.

At the *numbness* stage the helper will contribute most actively when he responds positively to the bereaved person's acceptance that their loved one has died. At the *searching* stage he will gently encourage the gradual realisation that the dead person is no longer to be found. At the stage of *disorganisation* he will stay with the bereaved's profound sadness as the reality of loss is finally accepted. At the final stage of *reorganisation* he will encourage the eventual discarding of a life-style built around the one who has died and the development of a new identity which embraces the once unimaginable possibility of life without the loved one. He will do all of this knowing that the stages are not neat compartments but that they will flow into each other almost imperceptibly and that the bereaved person may stray backwards and forwards between the stages.

All of this is not only very difficult but extremely risky. Danger lies in the fact that, at each stage, the helper will be siding with the impulse that the bereaved finds least congenial. Denial of what has to be faced or accomplished may appear a much more palatable option. At the *pining* stage particularly the helper may find herself at the receiving end of the bereaved person's misplaced anger if she is perceived as trying to end the 'search' prematurely. It is important therefore that the bereaved themselves set the pace. Nevertheless, the helper's 'bias' in accepting where the bereaved person is but also gently encouraging forward movement can be a vital element in the bereaved person's progress.

At the beginning of this chapter I raised the question of what the bereaved need from their helpers. Four answers have emerged from the psychological study of bereavement. The bereaved need:

(1) Permission and space to express their grief in a death-denying society;
(2) Attentive listening as they set their own pace through the grieving process;
(3) Willingness to share pain and not to block the process of grief by premature relief;
(4) Gentle encouragement of forward movement through the stages of grief towards eventual resolution.

The Role of the Clergy

The next question to be raised is whether and how well these needs are likely to be met from within the tradition of Christian faith and practice. Traditionally the church has ministered to the bereaved in two principal ways: the visitation of the clergy and the funeral service. It now remains to examine the effectiveness of these elements in the light of what we know of the experience of bereavement.

Visiting the Bereaved

In our society, despite encroaching secularisation, it is still regarded as normal in many quarters for the clergy to be involved in the support of the bereaved — not only of churchgoers but of others also. Parkes for one seems to welcome this tradition while, at the same time pointing out that not all clergy are necessarily well equipped for this task. He writes:

> It has been traditional in most churches for clergy to visit the sick and the bereaved, but the opportunity thus given to the clergy to become key figures in supporting the bereaved and in aiding the

transition from married person to widow or widower is seldom realized. Clergy, like everyone else, are often embarrassed and ineffectual when face to face with those who have been or are about to be bereaved.[12]

There can be no doubt that those writers on the psychology of bereavement who comment on what they have come across of the involvement of clergy in bereavement have found the quality patchy. This inevitably creates some cynicism. One pair of writers, for instance, remark:

> Possibly we have taken it for granted that religious educators know what to say in a crisis situation. However we must admit our dismay when a child has died and a clergyman has said to the parents, 'Your little girl was so good that God wanted her in Heaven.'[13]

It would be easy to make a collection of such horror stories. But what should the role of the clergy be in the eyes of those who specialize in the study of bereavement? Parkes, at least, makes some helpful suggestions:

> The role of the visiting clergyman is similar to that of any other friendly person who wishes the bereaved person well and would like to be of help. He too should be prepared to show by his manner acceptance of grief and particularly acceptance of the bitter anger against God that is likely to be expressed. He will not help matters by returning the anger, by meeting emotion with dogma or agony with glib assurance. He will help best by listening and, if invited to do so, by trying to collaborate with the bereaved person in an honest attempt to 'get things straight'.[14]

For Parkes then, the clergy will be most helpful to the bereaved when, like any other helper, they contribute to meeting the kind of needs outlined above. He sees two particular risks for clergy in this role, however. One is that they may well find themselves to be the recipients of anger directed either at God who has caused or allowed this death to take place or at themselves as God's representatives. The danger for clergy at this point is that they may attempt to become the defenders or justifiers of God — or become so offended that they return anger for anger. What we have learned about the place of anger in the grieving process should be enough to demonstrate how inappropriate such responses would be.

The other risk is that they may be tempted to use what Parkes calls 'dogma' to shore up a defensive position in relation to grief, denying the validity of emotion or offering assurance as a remedy for grief. It may at first sight appear, therefore, that the clergy's theology is their greatest disadvantage in the context of bereavement and this must raise the inevitable question as to whether they are the right people to be involved in counselling the bereaved at all!

In many churches, nowadays, there is movement towards the transfer of bereavement counselling to people other than those in ordained ministry. Where such people are adequately trained and supervised and where this is seen as extending the ministry of the church, rather than providing an alternative to spiritual support, this is a most healthy and helpful development. It may be, however, that behind this tendency there lurks, in some people's minds, the belief that the support of the bereaved should be undertaken by people whose training is in medicine, psychology or sociology rather than theology. This is to miss the point.

If help is truly to be given to bereaved people in a Christian context, then it is vital that those offering such help have not only a knowledge of the contemporary understanding of bereavement from a psychological perspective, such as has been outlined in this part of the book, but that also, as Christians, their understanding is backed up by a theology which is genuinely supportive of the process of grief. The choice for the Christian helper, lay or ordained, is not between a psychological or a theological approach to bereavement but between a theology that is supportive of or antithetical towards the grieving process.

The Funeral

The other point at which the bereaved person is likely to come into direct contact with the church is the funeral service. This is a function for which the church holds a quasi-monopoly in our society. Even those opting for the anonymity of a cremation unrelated to any church community are likely to be allotted a 'duty minister' to conduct the ceremony. It is more difficult to avoid than to encounter a representative of the Christian faith at this point.

In terms of the grieving process, the funeral service is likely to occur as the bereaved emerge from *numbness* into *yearning* or at an early point in the second stage. Its helpfulness to the grieving person will therefore be determined by how well it assists in the acknowledgement of the reality that death has taken place or gives opportunity for the expression of the emotions of grief. For several widows, says Parkes of one of his samples, 'it was the funeral service that "brought home" the reality of what had happened.'[15]

Clearly the various branches of the Christian church, under whose auspices the majority of funerals in Western society are conducted, bear great responsibility. At this point there exists a pastoral opportunity to make a substantial contribution to the movement towards the acceptance of reality or to reinforce denial on the basis of perceived Christian beliefs. At this point too, however, we are all subject to the dominant trends of our culture. Raphael reminds us of cultural variations with regard to the expectations of the funeral even within Europe:

> Some cultures expect and demand a very open expression of grief at the loss and would view as shameful a funeral where tears were not shed and emotion was hidden. Many European cultures, such as those of the Greeks and Italians, have quite clear expectations of open and strong emotional release; whereas Anglo-Saxon society may view such public display of feeling as unseemly, praising the person who shows strong emotional control.[16]

Psychological writers on bereavement stress the importance of the funeral service. None of them, of course, gives consideration to its theological content. However, there is a clear dilemma facing the church leader conducting a funeral service. The assumptions of our society and the expectations of many mourners encourage the use of the service for the reinforcement of denial. It is all too easy to choose words and practices from within the Christian tradition which collaborate with such expectations. If the funeral is to be of genuine help to the bereaved, however, it must facilitate the acceptance of reality and this may involve the acceptance of a freer expression of emotion than we are used to.

At the same time, if such a service is going to remain an act of worship, its content must not be simply psychologically motivated but must have also a firm theological basis. Ministers have often debated whether the funeral service should be shaped by the demands of Christian worship or the needs of mourners. This is to miss the point. People in grief will be best served by an act of worship based firmly on a Christian view of death which does not deny reality, which encourages the acceptance of loss, gives space for the expression of grief and yet holds out a hope based on the death and resurrection of Jesus Christ. A funeral service planned on that basis will be found to meet the psychological needs of mourners in the profoundest way.

Recapturing the Vision

This book has been written out of the conviction that the Christian church, including its ministers, has often let down the bereaved. This is being admitted by many nowadays, and because of this Christian ministers and others caring for the bereaved are often urged to supplement their Christian teaching about death with a psychological understanding of the grieving process. This is true but it is not enough. Christians have let down the bereaved not principally through a lack of psychology but through a misunderstanding of what should be their own teaching about life after death.

A misunderstanding of what the Bible really teaches in this area has convinced many that death is not real and that grief is an invalid emotion. The psychology of bereavement which has developed during this century has shown us where we have gone wrong in practice and helped us to see what it is that the grieving really need. However, it has only shown us what already ought to have been evident from the church's own tradition and theology.

The best way to help the grieving which has unfolded in this chapter from an examination of contemporary psychological understanding of the grieving process coincides with the logic of death and resurrection in the gospel. It is this that needs to be recaptured as the authentic vision of Christianity, not simply for the sake of a purer theology (important as that may be) but as a matter of urgent practical necessity for those experiencing the pain of bereavement — that is to say for all people at some point in their lives.

PART V
Christians and Bereavement Today

Chapter 11

CHRISTIANS, GRIEF AND AFTERLIFE

> The Bible teaches whether we are saved or lost, there is an everlasting existence of the soul.[1]

The tone of certainty is unmistakable. Billy Graham might have pronounced those words to some vast crowd in one of the great arenas of the world. In fact they come from his book *Facing Death and the Life After* in which the great evangelist looks at many aspects of death from a Christian perspective. He does not tell us where in the Bible he finds the idea of an immortal soul spelt out so clearly, or indeed what he means precisely by the phrase he uses.

Certainly when, elsewhere in the book, he depicts the bliss of the eternal state he uses language which recalls the experience of Augustine and his mother in the garden at Ostia:

> Have you ever said, 'I wish this moment could last forever?' I suspect those feelings are a small indication of what it would be like, frozen in time and loving God, enjoying him forever. We will never come down from that 'mountaintop' experience.[2]

Could it be that Billy Graham really sees eternity as a timeless moment of ecstasy, a Christian's 'mountaintop' experience lasting forever, 'frozen' bliss? To what extent is Billy Graham an Augustinian? No-one could, of course, accuse him, any more than Augustine himself, of not believing in the resurrection. This, however, is where he places the resurrection of the body in the final scheme of things:

> Death has two stages, first the separation of the body from the spirit of a person for a purely spiritual existence, and second, reunion with the body and a glorious resurrection at the Second Coming of Christ.[3]

In typical Augustinian fashion, resurrection is retained but relegated. It is awaited, perhaps, as a glorious consummation but is no longer — and this is what really counts — the grounds on which we are assured of eternal life. This is based simply on a separation of soul and body at a moment which we can, on this view, call only the death of the body.

This 'purely spiritual existence' of the intermediate state, however, seems to have some peculiar characteristics. For instance, 'the moment we take our last breath on earth we take our first in heaven.'[4] So our disembodied souls have physical qualities also! Similarly, using the Transfiguration as an example: 'The disciples recognized Moses and Elijah, although they did not yet have their resurrection bodies . . . They had recognisable bodies; they were not disembodied, ghostly apparitions.'[5] There seems not only to be an intermediate state but also intermediate bodies. It is difficult to understand, on this basis, precisely what difference the resurrection is going to make. Did Paul not speak about the 'spiritual body' as the form with which we should rise on the 'last day'? It seems here that such a rising could be dispensed with without any great loss.

I would like to make it clear that these inconsistencies are not being pointed out in any sense of disrespect to Billy Graham to whose preaching of the gospel many thousands of our generation of Christians owe their first stirrings of faith or a decisive moment of commitment. He is quoted here as the most pre-eminent spokesperson of evangelicalism of our age. If Billy Graham is confused then it is a confusion reflected in many other Christians of our generation.

However, because Dr. Graham's book on death covers practical as well as purely theological ideas, we have a rare opportunity to trace where this eschatological confusion leads in the thinking of a Christian. For example, when he writes about the experience of facing death we find a typical ambiguity. On the one hand, he deplores our 'death-denying society' and with impressive honesty he admits to his own reluctance to face death:

> Now I am not anxious to die . . . And just because the Bible tells us that believers have a blessed hope of conquering death, we don't run to the door and say to the enemy, 'Come on in, I've been waiting anxiously for you.' It is not a sign of weak faith for the Christian to face death with reluctance.[6]

The effect of this is somewhat neutralized later, however, when he says that Jesus 'has taken away the fear of death for those who trust in him.'[7] Indeed Jesus' own fear of death is to be explained by its unique atoning character. Only in this way will it bear comparison with the courage shown by Socrates who died only for himself. For this reason the comparison of the deaths of Jesus and Socrates leads to a very different conclusion than that reached by Oscar Cullmann.[8] We are left feeling unsure as to whether death should be feared or welcomed by a Christian.

Similar ambiguities arise in his treatment of grief. By and large this is dealt with realistically and compassionately with a description of the 'emotions of grief' and some helpful advice on being a comforter. Permission to grieve, however, seems to end at the funeral which 'should be a coronation ceremony, a statement to the world about eternal life'.[9] And we are let in on the Grahams' personal plans: 'Personally, Ruth and I know where we will be buried and we have expressed our desires to have a home-going "celebration", not a woeful wake.'[10] Once again we encounter the spirit of Aristeides.

What we discover here should not surprise us at this point in this book. Billy Graham's teaching stands as a paradigm of modern evangelicalism. Confusion in eschatology results in confusion over practical areas concerning death. Graham's strong biblicism and desire to retain a concept of resurrection, even when it is hard to find a place for it, creates a note of realism which allows the expression of some reluctance in facing death and the acknowledgement of the validity of grief up to a point. On the other hand, the inherited and unquestioned belief in an immortal soul and the logical consequence of this that death is not really death, rules out admission of the fear of death and when it comes to the public acknowledgement of death in a funeral service insists that grief be suppressed in the interests of 'celebration'.

A different view

Billy Graham's book gives us an excellent example of the 'two-tier' view of eternal life typical of much Christian thinking today. This view attempts to combine the biblical vision of resurrection and the Platonic view of an immortal soul with the latter retaining the decisive function of being the grounds on which hope for life beyond this one is based. Graham demonstrates for us the practical consequences of this in our approach to death and bereavement. We would be mistaken, however, to assume that this is only an evangelical problem.

As a touchstone of a more liberal yet still popular approach we might turn to Peter Mullen's book *Death Be Not Proud*[11]. Mullen, an Anglican priest, writer and broadcaster, concurs emphatically with the view of our society as a death-denying one. His favourite terms for denoting this are 'euphemism' and 'euphemistic' which he uses freely. In deploring this tendency and insisting upon our facing up to what he calls the 'horror-struck dereliction' of grief, he uses the language of resurrection:

> We were never promised that we would not be broken, really broken; but that we shall be put together again. After death the resurrection.[12]

Is Mullen then a resurrectionist, resisting the pull towards Platonic dualism? Not quite. Plato's view of immortality is to be taken seriously:

> For thousands of years mankind has believed that he possesses an immortal soul. It was not only so-called primitive people who believed this but Plato. Is Plato not deemed to be as intelligent as the Producer of Tomorrow's World or Q.E.D.?[13]

In fact: 'In Christian theology, the resurrection of the body means that the death of our physical members is not the end of us.'[10] What this means for Mullen is that 'the doctrine of immortality in the Christian incarnational tradition, is described as the resurrection of a body' because in it 'there is some persistence of substance and not of mere ideas'.[14] In the last analysis he admits that the doctrine of the 'the resurrection to eternal life solves nothing'[15] because of the philosophical problems which it raises. The long last section of his book is a rather poetic attempt to reinterpret resurrection in terms of art and nature. If these fail as comforts, 'There is morality and there is work'![16] It is not clear whether Mullen believes that these things constitute what resurrection *is*, but he concludes, significantly, if not totally consistently, 'The greatest and most reassuring comfort for me is in the Bible's psychological and spiritual realism.'[17]

I have quoted both Billy Graham and Peter Mullen at length

because, as two popular writers in two different theological traditions, we find them both struggling to create the same synthesis for the sake of ordinary Christians who want to understand the puzzling concept of life after death. Both, in their different ways, are attempting to construct a Christian eschatology out of two elements which ultimately do not fit very well together. Neither comes up with a synthesis which is totally coherent. If this is the background to popular Christian thinking today about the Christian hope of eternal life, it will be no surprise to find a corresponding confusion in the Christian view of bereavement. What will occupy us for the rest of this chapter will be the way this subject tends to be dealt with in the kind of popular paperbacks available on the shelves of Christian bookshops.

Christian Books on Bereavement

The first, and perhaps surprising thing to be discovered is that most Christian books on bereavement take their starting point, not so much from any theological perspective as from the psychological understanding of bereavement outlined in the last part of this book. Typically, the writer of a Christian book about bereavement is more likely to be a health professional or counsellor than a minister or theologian. This means that they tend to follow what I have called the Parkes-Bowlby approach to grief. In fact the most notable feature of Christian descriptive literature on bereavement is that it is a popularisation of more technical secular theory, often illustrated with anecdotes and case histories.

The style in which this is done of course varies. One book, for instance, while issued by a Christian publisher, is simply a socio-psychological handbook on bereavement with no religious content at all.[18] Another purports to have much more popular appeal claiming to be an 'everyday' treatment of the subject for 'common people'.[19] Some are based explicitly on Bowlby's attachment theory.[20] This tendency is demonstrated by the descriptions of grief symptoms[21] and the definition of grief as work.[22]

Prominent too are the lists of stages of grief.[23] These are sometimes extended by the inclusion of symptoms (anger, guilt etc.) as separate stages or are classified slightly differently, but essentially they follow the scheme set out in chapter 8 of this book. For example, one book's chapter headings are essentially

popularisations of the standard stages and symptoms in terms
of the sort of thing 'everyday' bereaved people might say:

> 'It couldn't happen to me.' (pre-bereavement)
> 'It hasn't happened to me.' (numbness/denial)
> 'It shouldn't have happened to me.' (anger)
> 'Why has it happened to me?' (questioning)
> 'I feel sad that it has happened to me' (realisation)
> 'I feel bad that it has happened to me.' (guilt)
> 'But it has happened to me.' (acceptance)
> 'I feel sort of glad that it has happened to me.' (healing)[24]

One booklet, designed for handing to bereaved people, gives a
potted account of the grieving process consisting of a rather
mechanical list of stages of grief, interwoven with the story of
Jesus at the tomb of Lazarus and set out between close-up
photographs of flowers.[25] Whatever else might be said about the
Christian literature of bereavement, it is usually soundly based
on psychological theory.

Having noted the general trend, however, it is interesting to
find, by way of contrast, this piece of advice from an American
couple, both widowed and now married to each other:

> Dealing with a severe crisis such as the death of a mate is softened
> to the degree that you bring your feelings and expectations in line
> with Jesus' teachings. That means waiting and trusting in God and
> his long range plan for your life. Learn a lesson from Job who sat
> on an ash heap for a period of time. To be spiritually alive and
> mentally productive, we all need to undergo some pruning and
> refining before we can experience victorious Christian living . . .
> The first step is to immerse yourself in the Word and believe it.[26]

The word 'mate' apparently is American for spouse, not collo-
quial English for friend! The authors later go on to such practical
matters as 'handling your finances' and discussing 'your sexual
interest and . . . preferences' with future potential 'mates'. After
all, 'one of the major challenges facing you as a survivor is how
to make each day rich with contentment and personal fulfilment'![27]

However, such confidence that the problems of bereavement
can be solved by a positive spiritual outlook is, to tell the truth,
rare in Christian books on bereavement. It might rather be said
that theological or spiritual reflection is minimal and is often

confined to separate sections and thus insulated from the main arguments.[28] Even in Ian Ainsworth-Smith and Peter Speck's helpful handbook for ministers, *Letting Go*, most spiritual comment is confined to two chapters.[29] What is said in such sections is variable. In one book six short pages optimistically entitled *Theology* seem to say little more than that different people will need different quantities of religious input in their bereavement.[30]

Many Christian writers, in fact, seem embarrassed by the ambiguities of their faith in the context of the apparent certainties of psychological research. They do not seem to know quite what to do with it. Some accept the possibility that bereavement could well result in a disturbing, albeit often temporary, loss of faith.[31] As one writer puts it:

> Many people testify to experiences that have come in the midst of desolation and pain, of a 'peace that passes understanding'. Yet for others no such comfort comes from God. In fact, for many faithful people, there are months, even years of feeling cut off from his comfort before it is found again.[32]

This uncertainty about the place of faith in the context of bereavement is especially evident when the area of belief in view is the question of life after death. Many Christian writers on bereavement treat this theme rather awkwardly, seeming unsure of how to fit it in with the general scenario of bereavement. Generally there is a feeling that it ought to be a positive contribution but also an uncertainty about how this is meant to operate.

Susan Wallbank, a CRUSE counsellor, writing firstly with the 'young adult' in mind, is optimistic about the hope for reunion as a resource in bereavement:

> The belief that we will definitely join up with the one who has died after our own death can take away some of the pain of bereavement because it brings hope for the future.[33]

She does not reflect however on what it might mean to have 'some of the pain' taken away or whether, in terms of the need to grieve fully, that is really desirable. In a later book dealing with sexual deprivation in bereavement, however, the same writer identifies an interesting complication created by the belief in life after death in the case of conjugal bereavement. How does the continued existence of a partner relate to the beginning of a new sexual relationship?

> How could we love, live with, or marry another person when still in a form of partnership with our first love? If we did remarry then would this new partner be with us in the life hereafter? If they were, would this create the difficulty of split loyalties between two loves? It is not unusual to ponder such deep and difficult thoughts in the quiet night hours.[34]

This of course is the question of the Sadducees in a contemporary and more sincere form. It will be remembered that Jesus answered the question by emphasising the changed relationships in the resurrection life, thus demonstrating precisely why the resurrection hope cannot and is not intended to be the kind of comfort many bereaved people would want it to be. The very raising of the question, however, throws doubt upon Wallbank's own confident statement in her earlier book.

Pat Wynnejones, in a book about children and bereavement lays stress on the hope of reunion as a means of mitigating the pain of childhood grief.[35] However, she also includes this telling comment from a correspondent:

> To a young child the idea of an eventual reunion is irrelevant — tomorrow is already an eternity away. Even for an adult it is here and now that one wants the loved one . . . I'm not sure that the idea of reunion is such a scriptural one — and I'm sure that spiritually it is very dangerous, especially for a child. It has to live its life in this world.[36]

Wynnejones herself adds rather ruefully, 'There is some truth in this.' Just how dangerous the appeal to the afterlife can be as a means of manipulating a child's emotions can be seen from this excerpt from a leaflet designed for bereaved children. Consider the hidden imperatives in this passage (my italics):

> That special part of a person, which the Bible calls 'the spirit', was taken from death to be with Jesus in Heaven . . . When a person dies, he or she cannot live with us here on earth. And that makes us sad. But because of Jesus that person can have life in heaven. *That should make us glad . . . It should also make us feel good* to know that, because we love and trust Jesus, we will be taken away from death to live with him and our family and friends in heaven.[37]

Jenifer Pardoe, another counsellor, experienced in hospice work, senses the potential traps hidden in a confident appeal to the afterlife as a resource for the bereaved:

> Many Christians will say, 'If my faith was strong enough, surely when someone dies, I should be full of joy for them. If I really believed then I would know they were in heaven, in eternal life, and I should be glad about that. Why don't I feel like that? What is this that I feel.'[38]

One has the impression, on reading these books, that some writers sense that the relationship between belief in life after death and bereavement is more complex than it might appear, but none of them tackles the issue head on. Perhaps this sense of unease explains why the subject attracts less attention than one might have expected.

Christian Ambivalence

Because most Christian writers on bereavement are people who have learned to care for the bereaved in a compassionate way and because their primary theoretical base is in a psychological understanding, they want to give the bereaved full permission to grieve and to express their grief openly. They seem unsure, however, how to relate this permission to Christian teaching.

The statement that 'Jesus wept' in John 11:35 is taken by many as a rather surprising acceptance of the need to grieve in the Bible and is seized on as a basis for encouraging Christians to allow themselves the freedom to shed tears. This, however, is often quoted in isolation and is not linked to any broader Christian view of why grief is an appropriate response. The need to grieve is generally kept in a separate category from the Christian hope of eternal life as if the two should not really be mentioned together.

There seems to be an underlying but unspoken theme in much of this literature which, if made explicit, could be expressed something like this:

> *Here are the facts about bereavement as encountered in human experience and elucidated by contemporary psychology. They teach us that grief is a natural phenomenon which is the normal human response to the loss of a loved one by*

death. We are not sure how this relates to the Christian faith which appears to be saying that death is not really a problem. In fact we feel rather embarrassed and apologetic about the whole thing. Nevertheless, we believe that, in spite of being a Christian and having a hope of everlasting life, you still have the human need to grieve and would encourage you to do so.

It is not only in books that such attitudes are hinted at. Many Christians struggle with relating their painful experience of grief to what they believe they ought to experience as a Christian. Grief is accepted apologetically and with varying degrees of guilt. Clearly such a position is preferable to one which denies Christians the freedom to grieve at all on the basis of a perceived understanding of Christian hope. Nevertheless it a very uncomfortable one and, moreover, unnecessary.

In order to come to terms with their grief, Christians do not need to hide from their Christian hope or to keep the two experiences in separate chapters of books or in different compartments of their lives. The experience of grief has always been congruent with the Christian hope of resurrection. When Christians have not felt this to be the case it is because they have misunderstood the basis of what we hope for or because that hope has been misplaced onto something other than the death and resurrection of Jesus Christ.

As an example of a Christian who affirms both the resurrection basis of hope and the need for realism in the face of suffering, I close this chapter with a comment from Elaine Storkey in a booklet designed for bereaved parents.

> For in his resurrection Jesus showed us that there is life after death and a life without pain. But for our suffering now the Christian message does not offer us easy solutions. It says rather the reverse, that this world is hard and life can be very difficult . . . Even God is affected by the world's sin. He chose to suffer the anguish of bereavement in order to bring hope to us. But it [the Christian hope] will not take the pain away. Jesus himself did not escape suffering.[39]

Chapter 12

THE CHRISTIAN AUTOBIOGRAPHY OF BEREAVEMENT: A CONTEMPORARY GENRE

Perhaps the most famous bereavement of the twentieth century in the English-speaking world is that of C.S. Lewis. That the story should be so well known is, in itself, remarkable enough. At the time of his wife's death Lewis was an aging academic who had lectured in English literature at Oxford and Cambridge. His fame, however, rested on his radio talks and popular books on Christian theology and morality and particularly on his series of allegorical fantasy writings for children, the *Narnia* stories. He had been a bachelor most of his life and had married Joy Davidman, a divorced American poet, at her hospital bed where she was shortly expected to die of cancer. Joy experienced a period of remission during which the couple enjoyed a brief taste of married bliss before Joy's eventual death in 1960.

The reason we know so much about C.S. Lewis' experience of grief is that during the first year of his bereavement he kept a notebook of jottings in which he recorded his feelings with outstanding honesty. This was later published under the pseudonym of N.W. Clerk with the title, *A Grief Observed*.[1]

The book and the circumstances in which it was written were the inspiration for a television film called *Shadowlands* by William Nicholson, subsequently adapted as a West End theatre play and then as a film which became a surprising box-office success.[2] The title *Shadowlands* comes from the last of the Narnia books, *The Last Battle*, which recounts the eschatology of Lewis' imaginary world. At the end of this book, the lion Aslan, a character who throughout the series of stories represents the figure of Christ, says:

> Have you not guessed? . . . all of you are — as you used to call it
> in the Shadowlands — dead. The term is over; the holidays have
> begun. The dream is ended; this is the morning.[3]

The term *Shadowlands* therefore represents the insubstantial
nature of this life compared to the solidity of the next.[4]

The Last Battle was first published four years before Joy's
death and shortly before her diagnosis as having cancer. This
demonstrates that the idea of life after death was already exer-
cising Lewis's thinking before these events. It is therefore all the
more fascinating to find the following little exchange between
the characters on the subject of grief. As the children in the story
move from the dying world of Narnia and before they have
discovered the delights which await them, one of them, Lucy, is
scolded by her older brother for weeping. She replies:

> Don't try to stop me, Peter . . . I am sure Aslan would not. I am
> sure it is not wrong to mourn for Narnia. Think of all that lies dead
> and frozen behind that door.

Another, Narnian, character supports her:

> Sirs, . . . The ladies do well to weep. See, I do so myself. I have
> seen my mother's death. What world but Narnia have I ever
> known? It were no virtue, but great discourtesy, if we did not
> mourn.[5]

Before he describes his mythological heaven, therefore, Lewis
seems to want to grant permission to grieve for the end of this
life. This is an important detail since it demonstrates that the
need to grieve was not something that Lewis submitted to *in spite
of* his beliefs but that it was already a coherent part of his
theology. It may be that the metaphorical reference to 'my
mother's death' relates to Lewis' loss of his mother as a young
child which, as he describes it in the autobiographical account
of his early life, was clearly very traumatic, in fact the end of 'all
settled happiness'.[6]

Before turning to *A Grief Observed* to follow the course of
Lewis' grief it will be helpful to know what is the theological basis
for Lewis' strong affirmation of the validity of grief. He leaves us
in no doubt about this in one of his previous books, *Miracles*.

Here he states categorically:

> the Resurrection was not regarded simply or chiefly as evidence
> for the immortality of the soul. It is of course often so regarded
> today: I have heard a man maintain that 'the importance of the
> resurrection is that it proves *survival*'. Such a view cannot at any
> point be reconciled with the language of the New Testament.[7]

In view of some opinions quoted earlier in this book, it is
interesting also to read the following words from Lewis: 'It must
be clearly understood that if the Psychical Researchers suc-
ceeded in proving "survival" and showed that the Resurrection
was an instance of it, they would not be supporting the Christian
faith but refuting it.' The only view of life after death that the
resurrection of Christ can be said to support, according to C.S.
Lewis, is the Hebraic-apocalyptic view of the resurrection of the
righteous dead.[8] As we come to read Lewis' personal account of
his own bereavement it is important to realize that we are reading
the experience of a man who had rejected the concept of the
survival of the immortal soul and whose view of the Christian
hope was in terms of death and resurrection.[9]

A Grief Observed

It is possible that the opening words of *A Grief Observed* are
the most frequently quoted in modern Christian literature on
bereavement.

> No one ever told me that grief felt so like fear. I am not afraid,
> but the sensation is like being afraid. The same fluttering in the
> stomach, the same restlessness, the yawning. I keep on swallow-
> ing.

This is how C.S. Lewis describes the first pangs of his grief. What
follows can easily be recognized as a very graphic description of
the stage of numbness and shock.

> At other times it feels like being mildly drunk, or concussed. There
> is a sort of invisible blanket between the world and me.[10]

As we might expect, this feeling soon gives way to an urge to
conjure up the memory of Joy. Bowlby and Parkes would have
called this the beginning of the phase of searching and pining.

Here and throughout the book Joy is referred to by the initial H from her first name, Helen. He firmly resists any temptation to sentimentalize her memory.

> For H. wasn't like that at all. Her mind was lithe and quick and muscular as a leopard. Passion, tenderness and pain were all equally unable to disarm it. It scented the first whiff of cant or slush; then sprang, and knocked you over before you knew what was happening. How many bubbles of mine she pricked![11]

One fascinating thing about this book from a Christian perspective is the way that Lewis seeks to integrate his painful experience with his theology. Impressively the great Christian moralist succeeds in being totally honest about his feelings with regard to God. The first thing he notes is a sense of God's absence.

> Meanwhile, where is God? . . . Go to Him when your need is desperate, when all other help is vain, and what do you find? A door slammed in your face, and a sound of bolting and double-bolting on the inside. After that, silence. You may as well turn away. The longer you wait the more emphatic the silence will become.[12]

Soon, however, more disturbing thoughts are beginning to form:

> Not that I am (I think) in much danger of ceasing to believe in God. The real danger is of coming to believe such dreadful things about him. The conclusion I dread is not, 'So there's no God after all,' but, 'So this is what God's really like. Deceive yourself no longer.'[13]

Later, these thoughts start to take a more explicit shape. The thought that God has a purpose in suffering does not bring comfort but its opposite. Suppose God is experimenting with us like rats in a trap. 'Supposing the truth were "God always vivisects?" ' or that he is really 'The Cosmic Sadist'?[14]

Similarly, ideas of life after death bring little comfort. The beloved is not here. Whatever may happen in the future is not going to be the same as what was lost. Neither God nor Nature is 'a clown who whips away your bowl of soup one moment in order, next moment, to replace it with another bowl of the same soup.' Resurrection means change which gives space for grief.

> It is hard to have patience with people who say, 'There is no death,' or, 'Death doesn't matter'. There is death. And whatever

is matters. And whatever happens has consequences, and it and they are irrevocable and irreversible . . . I look up in the night sky. Is anything more certain than that in all those vast times and spaces, if I were allowed to search them, I should nowhere find her face, her voice, her touch? She died. She is dead. Is the word so difficult to learn?[15]

In a remarkable passage Lewis demonstrates why it is that, in the searching phase particularly, the doctrine of resurrection, properly understood, cannot be the comfort we might wish, and also how this contrasts with some immortality models, represented here by spiritualism.

Talk to me about the truth of religion and I'll listen gladly. Talk to me about the duty of religion and I'll listen submissively. But don't come talking to me about the consolations of religion or I shall suspect you don't understand. Unless, of course, you can literally believe all that stuff about family reunions 'on the further shore', pictured in entirely earthly terms. But that is all unscriptural, all out of bad hymns and lithographs. There's not a word of it in the Bible. And it rings false. We *know* it couldn't be like that. Reality never repeats. The exact same thing is never taken away and given back. How well the Spiritualists bait their hook! 'Things on this side are not so different after all.' There are cigars in Heaven. For that is what we should all like. The happy past restored.[16]

Eventually, of course, Lewis's intense pining gives way to profound sadness. He finds that he is not thinking of 'H' all the time now but is constantly pervaded by a sense of unease, of 'wrongness'. The most unlikely things appear 'depressing'.[17] No longer plagued by the same terrifying thoughts about God, he senses guilt for what he thought and doubts if his faith was ever real.[18] Sometimes, he feels he might be 'getting over it'[19] but then comes the feeling that 'all the hells of young grief have opened again.'[20]

However, there is forward movement. He goes for a walk visiting familiar haunts where, instead of looking 'emptied of its beauty' as before, the scenery invites him to 'a past kind of happiness, my pre-H happiness.' He refuses the invitation: 'I don't want to go back and be happy in that way.'[21] A new identity is beginning to form. A turning point is the following, famous experience:

> Imagine a man in total darkness. He thinks he is in a cellar or dungeon. Then there comes a sound. He thinks it might be a sound from far off — waves or wind-blown trees or cattle half a mile away. And if so it proves he is not in a cellar, but free, in the open air. Or it may be a much smaller sound close at hand — a chuckle of laughter. And if so, there is a friend just beside him in the dark. Either way, a good, good sound.[22]

As Lewis continues, from this point on, to reflect on his experience, he does so with a greater sense of serenity. Not that there is absence of pain or that he has adopted glib answers but that new reality is being accepted. 'All reality is iconoclastic . . . Not my idea of God, but God. Not my idea of H, but H.'[23]

Towards the end of the book he records an experience in which he seemed to sense Joy's presence as a mental image. This leads him to toy with the idea of 'sheer intellects' and comments, 'A Greek philosopher wouldn't have been surprised at an experience like mine'.[24] It is the thought of resurrection, however, which pulls him back:

> There is also, whatever it means, the resurrection of the body. We cannot understand. The best is perhaps what we understand least.[25]

Reading *A Grief Observed* with a knowledge of bereavement theory, we watch C.S. Lewis pass through all the classic textbook symptoms of grief. The remarkable fact is that he records the process of grief before the textbooks were written! He could hardly have been influenced by what was to become the psychological understanding of bereavement and yet, in Parkes' or Bowlby's terms, Lewis' grief was a prime specimen which could easily have been used to illustrate their manuals.

This may be a welcome confirmation of psychological theory but this is not my point. Here we find a highly intelligent and articulate Christian describing his grief in a refreshingly honest and uninhibited way. Lewis demonstrates what healthy grief is like in all its pain and hard labour. In Lewis, as in the biblical examples in the first part of this book, we find that a belief in death and resurrection is perfectly compatible with the full expression of grief.

A Severe Mercy

C.S. Lewis is important for the Christian understanding of bereavement not only in his own right but also because of what he started. The popularity of *A Grief Observed* has, in a remarkable way, given Christians permission to talk about their own grief. It has sparked off in recent decades what can be regarded as a genre: the depiction of grief by individual Christians and its interpretation in the light of what is understood as Christian teaching. It is fascinating to observe, what has become of this legacy from C.S. Lewis in the hands of others.

Perhaps the first of these autobiographical accounts, and one which claims to stand in succession to Lewis, is Sheldon Vanauken's story of his love and grief, *A Severe Mercy*.[26] Vanauken was much influenced by Lewis; he and his wife 'Davy' came to Christian faith in Oxford partly through Lewis's influence and the book contains 25 letters or fragments of letters from Lewis to Vanauken, some of which coincide with Lewis's own marriage and bereavement. Although written considerably later, the book was inspired by *A Grief Observed*. It therefore gives us a unique opportunity to see what happens to the Lewis heritage as it is translated by a less acute mind and a very different human experience.

Unlike Lewis, Vanauken spends a good deal of the book dealing with the development of his love affair and marriage. This occurs in the privileged atmosphere of wealthy, upper middle-class American society. The couple resolved from the start to 'keep the magic of inloveness' by nurturing 'closeness' and erecting around their relationship a 'shining barrier'.[27] Considerable space is given too to the account of conversion and the potential threat of faith in God to the exclusivism of their mutual adoration.[28]

It is, however, the way Vanauken deals with his grief that is of interest here. When Davy died, he felt assured that 'past faith and belief . . . she herself — her soul — still was.' No funeral took place; he scattered her ashes himself in a churchyard with romantic memories.[29]

In describing his subsequent grief Vanauken attempts, like Lewis, to be totally frank and self-revealing. The result, however, gives the impression of being too self-conscious, romanticized and lacking in Lewis's characteristic self-restraint. It often seems to be saying more about the postures of grief which Vanauken *chose* to take up than about the symptoms of grief which overtook him. It is by no means as free as Lewis's account from denial. The first sixty letters he wrote all ended: 'And in Davy's words: "All shall be most well." '[30]

The most remarkable feature of his handling of grief is an experiment which he called the 'Illumination of the Past'[31] in which he set about deliberately to relive each memory of their shared existence. In a manner of which Freud would have been proud he 'hypercathected' each strand of libido:

> As I went through the past, day by day, ten thousand forgotten or half-forgotten memories of Davy came to me with all the colour and vividness of life. For one instant *that* particular Davy — gay or mocking or inquisitive or adventurous or loving — stands before me, warm and real and alive. I respond to her with a surge of love and pure joy. That is followed an instant later by the awful awareness that *this* Davy, too, is dead. Then, irresistibly, come the tears — the tears for this particular Davy. Until now *she* has not been touched by death — and she, too, must die. On the day following, if I reread that bit of the Journal, she will not stand before me: there will be no tears. Each memory calls forth warm, living reality *once*: it is followed by another little death and the tears.[32]

Another striking feature of this grief was the strong sense of Davy's presence. This seems to culminate in two experiences after about two years of bereavement. He claims that the clarity of the first of these placed it beyond normal dreams. It is implied that this was, in some way, a real 'visitation' to give him the assurance of the reality of Davy's presence:

> 'Are you — well, *with* me sometimes? I've sometimes thought you might be.'
> 'Yes, I am,' she said, 'I know all your doings.'
> 'Thank God,' I said, . . . 'And my letters to you — have you, um, read them? Over my shoulder maybe?'
> . . . . 'Yes, dearling, I've read them all.'[33]

The second experience involved the eventual 'departure' of Davy. He sensed the nearness and then the withdrawal of his wife. He seems to interpret this quite objectively: 'the disappearance of the beloved's presence and, therefore, the end of tears'. However, 'The disappearance of the grief is not followed by happiness. It is followed by emptiness.'[34]

It is interesting to observe Lewis's attitude to all this, most of which happened prior to or just after Joy's death. Vanauken portrays Lewis as a close and sympathetic friend which, no doubt, he was. There are hints in the letters, however, that Lewis did not approve of Vanauken's indulgence. A particularly revealing letter is one dated 8th May, 1955. Lewis had returned a 'wonderfully clear and beautiful' letter by Vanauken, asking him to reread it until 'you will in the end think as I do . . . about a life so wholly devoted to US.' He comments, 'One way or another the thing had to die.' It is in this context that Lewis describes the death of Davy in the phrase which became the title of the book: 'You have been treated with a severe mercy.'[35] Although Vanauken subsequently reflects on the meaning of this letter he does not seem to have got Lewis' message.

Although clearly intended to be in the Lewis tradition the depiction of grief in this book could hardly be farther in spirit from *A Grief Observed*. Undergirded by an immortalist, indeed almost spiritualistic, approach to life after death, it is self-indulgent and, although moving in places, smacks of posturing and unreality. One is left with the impression of a grief which, although romantic, is fundamentally unhealthy. Its importance lies in the fact that it provides an alternative model for subsequent attempts by Christians to describe their grief. From this point on Christian autobiographical accounts of bereavement have tended to follow one or other of these precedents.

Other Autobiographies

Within the last decade there has been an explosion of such writing. Almost any Christian bookshop these days will have a shelf dedicated to the subject of bereavement and most of the books on it will be autobiographical in style. Any attempt to catalogue them all would very quickly become out of date. These are the books that Christian bereaved people or their friends and carers are most likely to pick up and read. They both reflect and influence the way that Christian people today feel and think about their bereavement.

All of these writers are, no doubt, recounting their personal experience in a sincere way. They are often extremely moving to read. They are also, for the most part, genuinely struggling to interpret their experiences in the light of their Christian faith. It is tempting to see these factors as placing them beyond criticism. However, what is at stake here is not personal sincerity or good intentions but the effect of underlying assumptions and theological interpretations of experiences on the grieving process. The experiences described in these books are very painful and many of them are made even more painful because of the theological attitudes involved.

How can the value of such books be assessed in terms of their real helpfulness in the grieving process. One useful criterion is to look at them in the light of the 'Lewis' and 'Vanauken' models of bereavement autobiography. That is to say, to what extent in these books does a 'resurrectionist' theology lead to an acceptance of the need to grieve and a healthy passage through grief or to what extent do 'immortalist' assumptions block the grieving process? We can only look at a very small sample of the dozens of accounts written in English in the past decade.

Immortalist Autobiographies

Freda Baker, a journalist and writer, was widowed after a long and happy marriage. Like C.S. Lewis and many others since, she kept a journal of her feelings during the first year of bereavement which was subsequently published in the hope it would be of help to others in a similar situation. It is a frank, honest and very moving account. However, there are one or two things which give concern about Freda's experience as a contemporary model of grief.

One striking thing about her story is her strong sense of the continuing presence of her husband, Eric. We have seen that this, even when it includes hallucinatory experiences from time to time, is perfectly normal in bereavement. It is a way in which our mind 'finds a match' during the phase of 'searching' and it can sometimes be a brief temporary mitigation of pain which can be of help when it is recognized for what it is. In Freda's case, however, her view of life after death leads her to interpret these experiences in a literal way which, as in the case of Vanauken, verges on the spiritualistic:

> I think you were with me in the butcher's today . . . Knock on the door — nobody there . . . I expect you do come sometimes . . . I so often 'see' you going in and out. Passing through the kitchen, saying, 'All right then?' I slit a leek and you say, 'Mind how you go with that knife.'[36]

Not only are these experiences taken seriously but they start to form the basis of a sort of theological explanation of what happens to 'souls'. Like Vanauken, Freda feels that there is a moment when Eric 'departs':

> You are on a different wavelength now. That is why you have vanished as far as this world is concerned . . . Where you are now is where we came from in our source — our real home . . . Your world is invisible to us because of the different dimension. *That's all it is.*[37]

It is interesting to note that Freda's experience of Eric's 'immortal soul' has led her thinking in the same direction as Plato's. The state of disembodied eternity is our 'source' as well as the home to which we travel after death. She believes not only in the immortality of souls but in their pre-existence. The theology is not quite consistent, however, because after going to inhabit his new dimension, Eric still manages to get through sometimes: 'You came to me last night . . . Your voice actually came through to me. For a moment the wavelengths must have merged . . . I am stronger now.'[38]

One implication of all this, however, might now be predictable. If Eric is happy in heaven, the true home of his soul, and is, furthermore, able to communicate from there, then Freda's own feelings of grief are illicit. She has no reason to grieve:

> So knowing you are transported to great happiness and even watching over me to help me, why should I be sad?[39]

Symptoms of grief therefore have to be dealt with. They must be fought off with with the power of positive thinking. The following statement is one of many: 'Little by little, I must root out the unwanted anxiety by sending down into my subconscious the reassurance of positive thoughts.'[40] What we encounter in Freda Baker's story is a contemporary example of an ancient pattern. The immortality of the soul is used as a basis for the denial of grief.

Rosalind Allen's account of the death of her little daughter, Penelope as a result of a brain tumour is part of a collection of Christian bereavement stories edited by Ann Warren. The mother's perception of what was happening as Penelope died reveals a completely Platonic view of death. Perhaps the reference to floating near the ceiling comes from current accounts of near-death experiences which we have seen to be a modern form of the belief in immortality.

> As I kissed her I was aware of the real little person blithely floating away above me in the region of the ceiling . . . She was pausing on her cheery way, concerned to see me all alone and distressed by the form on the bed. I was filled with a great yearning to will her back. But it really felt as if God had spoken to me and although everything was finalized, Penelope's life would never finish . . . I bent to kiss the body, and suddenly realized that the chill flesh was merely a cast-off. Penelope was somewhere else altogether.[41]

Denial of what was happening was therefore immediate. Penelope was 'on her cheery way'; her body was only a cast-off; God had spoken; there was no real need to grieve.

However, further confirmation was obviously necessary. It came the following Sunday as the parents knelt in church. At the door appeared Penelope 'swinging on the arm of a tall, athletic eastern man at whose face I dared not look.' In case anyone should be suspicious about the authenticity of this vision, we are assured it could not have been 'wishful thinking' because it was 'in sharp contrast to my own feelings and the drear of that January morning.' After such assurances that Penelope was not really dead, the funeral was planned as 'a celebration of Penelope's last birthday on earth, her first in heaven.'[42]

We are not told of any future visions of Penelope. Nevertheless, the subsequent description of bereavement bears all the hallmarks of continuing denial. In public, Allen maintains a defiant refusal to grieve. She insists that she is 'at peace, knowing Penelope was being loved far better than she could have been by any of us.' Consider, however, in the words that follow, not only the deception of others but the self-deception and self-blame at repressed grief. One cannot help being reminded of Augustine:

> Yet I knew that I had to declare that fact (that she was at peace), in the face of all the tears I shed — frequently at night. During the

hours from midnight until three I was beset by doubt . . . by day, the tears were recognized as tears of deprivation . . . I knew that, in a sense, those tears are very selfish.[43]

Grief is, as it was for Plato and Augustine, something of which to be ashamed, to be expressed reluctantly and secretly in the dark hours. Even here they are reason for guilt and self-doubt. In daylight there has to be submission to the stern demands of a 'witness' to a belief which denies the reality of death and the need to grieve.

Resurrectionist Autobiographies

There are, however, personal accounts of grief which contrast with this tendency. **Robert Dykstra** is an American pastor whose wife, suffering from a clinical depression, committed suicide. Despite a foreword by Norman Vincent Peale of *The Power of Positive Thinking* fame, Dykstra makes no attempt to suppress the reality of his grief with positive thoughts. He writes:

She is gone. Death always comes in the Past Perfect tense. The action is completed, over and done. And I am alone, desperately alone. The initial shock and stunning unbelief are giving way to the deep, abiding sorrow of absence.[44]

In Dykstra this honesty of feeling is associated with strong statements about the horror of death[45] and about absolute dependence upon the concept of resurrection for any future hope.

When she died something in me — something fundamentally me — died too. And I can't get it back or revive it. I can only wait and hope for resurrection, for rebirth, for the long-expected day with Simeon.[46]

Dykstra like C.S. Lewis did not at first find any close sense of the presence of God to comfort him. Rather, he says, 'The silence of God is part of my sorrow.'[47] Nor did he find the comfort he might have expected in thoughts of heaven:

Death defies all our deepest spiritual imagery. The promise of a future heavenly home takes a back seat to the harsh present homesickness. I can't talk or think about heaven until I've dealt firmly and courageously with the finality of her physical death.[48]

He goes on to state significantly that this very frustration of imagery is a 'renewal of faith and hope.' He is thrown back upon the promises of God because, 'Neither a Cartesian description of heaven, nor an empirical proof for life beyond death can constitute our hope.'[49]

Dykstra also encounters the typical Christian urge to find purpose in all events — even in the death of those we love. His response however goes beyond the need for this kind of 'understanding'.

> I am tempted to discover miracles worked by her death. But they are mostly delusions and really add no significance to her dying.[50]

Later, he wonders whether the experience of grief he is enduring is going to equip him to be a more effective minister, but concludes,

> All that I know is that this son of Levi is going through the fire and whether he is going to be a better pastor for it remains questionable and, furthermore, irrelevant . . . It is simply his fire.[51]

Dykstra's model of life after death is expressed clearly in terms of death and resurrection. He acknowledges the reality and the awfulness of death and the pain of his own experience. He is neither ashamed nor afraid to grieve.

Another book which, in a remarkable way, combines a clear resurrectionist theology with a frank and non-evasive account of grief is **Nicholas Wolterstorff's** *Lament for a Son*. Clearly influenced by C.S. Lewis, Wolterstorff, a philosophy lecturer at Yale University, follows the 'journal' style of writing from the announcement of his twenty-five-year-old son's death in a mountaineering accident, to a visit to his graveside a year after the funeral.

Wolterstorff's short book deals with many vital themes in bereavement, some of which have been touched on in this book: the difficulty, at death, of conceptually separating person from body; the sense of numbness on hearing the news and pain as the numbness clears; the pressure particularly upon men not to cry; the importance for the bereaved of memory; anger at those who attempt to console by minimizing death; the real value of the funeral; the avoidance of grief in many books about grief; agnosticism about God's intentions; the solidarity of God with human suffering.[52]

Throughout these themes there runs the motif of resurrection. This comes to the fore in the following passage which I quote at length because of its relevance to all that I have been saying:

> Elements of the gospel which I had always thought would console did not. They did something else, something important, but not that. It did not console me to be reminded of the hope of resurrection. If I had forgotten that hope it would indeed have brought light into my life to have been reminded of it. But I did not think of death as a bottomless pit. I did not grieve as one who has no hope. Yet Eric is gone; *here* and *now* he is gone; *now* I cannot talk with him, *now* I cannot see him; *now* I cannot hug him; *now* I cannot hear of his plans for the future. *That* is my sorrow. A friend said, 'Remember he is in good hands.' I was deeply moved. But that reality does not put Eric back in my hands now. That's my grief. For that grief what consolation can there be other than having him back.
>
> In our day we have come to see again some dimensions of the Bible overlooked for centuries. We have come to see its affirmation of the goodness of creation. God made us embodied historical creatures and affirmed the goodness of that. We are not to yearn for timeless disembodiment.
>
> But this makes death all the more difficult to live with. When death is no longer seen as release from this miserable materiality, when death is seen rather as the slicing off of what God has declared to be, and what all of us feel to be, of great worth, then death is — well, not friend but enemy. Though I shall indeed recall that death is being overcome, my grief is that death still stalks this world and one day knifed down my Eric.[53]

Wolterstorff makes a number of points here which are worth spelling out: (1) resurrection does not offer consolation to the grieving; (2) grief is based on the pain of separation which hope does not answer; (3) the reason for this is linked with the (currently being recovered) biblical affirmation of embodiment; (4) death is still an enemy.

In Wolterstorff we encounter a Christian describing his grief without any mitigation on the grounds of his Christian faith. His account is credible both in terms of human experience and Christian theology. He achieves this synthesis on the basis of a properly understood doctrine of resurrection.

What we have discovered in contemporary bereavement autobiography comes as no surprise. Baker and Allen, Dykstra and

Wolterstorff are not isolated accounts; they serve simply as examples of two distinct Christian orientations to bereavement. We can see their prototypes in C.S. Lewis and Sheldon Vanauken. But the distinction is much more ancient. These two ways of encountering loss through death are as old and as far apart as the Bible and Platonic Greek philosophy.

Chapter 13

A THEOLOGY OF GRIEF?

Why do Christians find it hard to grieve? The title of this book is a question which has already been answered implicitly. It is time, however, to spell out the answer to the question in clear terms.

Christians find it hard to grieve because, like everyone else, they have an inbuilt tendency to deny the truth about death. Human beings fear death and cover their fear with denial. We want to believe in our own immortality. The death of someone close to us is a powerful reminder of what we want to avoid. It is a loss we would rather not recognize. We would rather believe that the impression of loss is illusory or that it is only temporary or that the powerful emotions that grip us are unnecessary and can be shrugged off with positive thinking.

Grief is unpleasant because, among other things, it involves the eventual acceptance of a loss including the loss of illusions about ourselves and our own lives. It is hard and painful work. We would rather do without it, but the hard facts of life force upon us the process towards acceptance which is, in reality, for our good and part of our healing. Such is the human condition. It is a condition in which Christians share.

But, why do *Christians* find it hard to grieve? That is – any more than anyone else? The Christian gospel has at its heart the affirmation that Jesus Christ defeated death. He defeated it by direct confrontation – not by avoidance, denial or, like the heroes of some of the world's folk stories, by trickery and deceit. Christ died and rose again. It was a death, moreover, from which the man Jesus, who was also the Son of God, shrank in repulsion. Not merely because of the particular physical horror of death by crucifixion, nor, as many have affirmed, only because of the representative nature of Christ's sacrifice, but as the paradigmatic Human Being in the face of 'the last enemy to be defeated'.

Jesus trembled on the brink of the nihilistic abyss and made explicit the fear which we all deny. And he died. He died, as the gospels tell us, if we can bear the shock of hearing it, without even the comforting sense of God's presence but with a feeling of having been totally abandoned. Yet it was not a despairing death. It was a death died in trust. That is why we can accept the almost contradictory words of Jesus from the cross recorded in all four gospels. But it is vital that we understand the grounds of Jesus' trust as he died. His trust did not lie in a belief in himself as immortal in respect of his humanity. Nor did it lie in a sense of personal immortality based upon his divine nature.

Jesus died trusting in the power and love of his Father, the Creator and giver of life, who could and would raise the dead to life again. This trust, as we have seen, stands in a stream of teaching about life, death and God stretching back into the ancient Scriptures. As it is put by that great Hebrew writer who had grasped so clearly the radical truth of the good news about Jesus: 'During the days of his flesh, he offered up prayers and petitions with loud cries and tears to the one who could save him out of death and he was heard because of his godliness' (Hebrews 5:7).

It is the consistent teaching of the New Testament that the death and resurrection of Jesus are the sign and pattern of our own. This is the Christian hope. It is based not upon a denial of death but the hope (in the strong meaning of the New Testament *elpis*) that through and beyond death God, who has pledged his love to us in Jesus, will raise us from the dead. It is a promise made not to a part of us but to the whole of our humanity.

Because in the gospel there is no denial of death, because our enemy is not avoided but engaged and overcome, there is not any hint either of a denial of the loss which death brings nor the human need to grieve. So, neither Jesus nor those to whom he entrusted the handing on of his message attempt any modification of the Old Testament tradition of giving vent to the emotions of grief. When Jesus stands in a crowd of mourners he adds his tears and his expressions of grief and anger to theirs; when risen from the dead he gives his followers space to grieve before revealing the glory of his resurrection. So, the members of the earliest Christian community 'mourn deeply' when one of them meets a violent death; the great apostle undergirds the experience of a mourning church with hope but does not deny their grief.

The gospel then contains resources to help Christians to grieve. More than others, the disciples of Jesus should be able to face the reality of death, their own and that of their loved ones, understand its nihilistic impact and approach it as did Jesus with both fear and hope, trusting not in any attribute of their humanity but in the power and promise of God. In understanding this, one might expect Christians to have the courage to face also the full pangs of grief, to endure the 'little death' of the loss of one of their loved ones, abandoning themselves to its pain until the 'little resurrection' of the eventual emergence of what the psychologists have called a 'new identity'.

There is nothing in the New Testament gospel of Jesus to make grief harder for Christians than for others – only resources to help them understand it, to put it into a meaningful theological context, and to sustain them through it by means of hope of resurrection. Many have discovered these resources and have received from them the courage to grieve honestly and authentically. But sadly, for others this has not been the case. Some Christians find the interface between their faith in Christ and the painful experience of bereavement a very uncomfortable area. Instead of finding their faith to be a resource they have encountered it as a complicating factor or a reason for denying the validity of their own experience.

So, *why* do Christians find it hard to grieve? Because so many have been seduced by what seemed to be a great historical shortcut in the grieving process that has proved to be only a path into a maze of pathological grief. Very early in the history of Christianity there was offered to Christians a way of sidestepping the pattern of death and resurrection. This offer emerged from the environment of Greek philosophy in which the early church had to make its presence felt. It came in the form of the Neoplatonic doctrine of the natural immortality of the soul.

The logic of immortality is that death is not real but an illusion. The death of the body is the release of the soul from physical limitations. One implication of such an idea is that grief is unnecessary, undesirable, evidence only of the weakness of the body. We have seen the 'shame' of grief not only in the pagan

Plato but in the second–century Christian community of Athens, in the newly converted Augustine and in contemporary 'immortalist' Christians.

'Immortality' in this sense has become so accepted as a Christian doctrine that many Christians are shocked at the suggestion that the immortality of the soul is not a biblical idea. Because the biblical evidence for the resurrection is so unmistakeable, what is commonly taken to be the 'Christian view of life after death' is an attempted synthesis of the two ideas. Our souls are released at death to enjoy or endure a temporary period of disembodiment before being joined again to a body at the resurrection at the end of time. Resurrection then becomes an ambivalent return to materiality whose desirability is open to question. It has certainly ceased to be, as it was for Jesus and Paul, the grounds for hope that the end of this life does not mean that God has finished with us. We are, in any case, on this view, immortal beings.

On this view, also, the experience of grief is equally questionable. Death is still only a transition – 'nothing at all'. Our loved ones, it is said, are only 'in another place', perhaps thought of, even by Christians, as still available to us. Grief is therefore inconsistent, a selfish indulgence of our own emotions when what we should be experiencing is a sense of joy for the bliss of those we only seem to have lost. For many Christians today the ancient logic of immortalism chimes in with the triumphalistic ideas of a Christianity that seeks to raise its adherents beyond the common problems of life on the basis of the so-called 'promises' of God.

While Christianity has historically, in so many of its forms, opted for this kind of avoidance of the truth about death and the human need to grieve, those involved in the world of secular psychology have, during the past century, looked many truths in the eye and plotted for us what seems to be a fairly reliable account of what it means, in human terms, to grieve for the death of a loved one. Many Christians who have known and reflected upon the experience of grief or whose work has led them into the care of grieving people have accepted the verdict of the psychologists but have found it difficult to integrate this with what they assume to be Christian teaching.

Christians today are sometimes counselled that they must grieve or that they have permission to grieve *despite* what they believe. A rift thus opens up between theology and experience. It is no surprise that, despite reassuring words, some Christians feel a sense of unease about following such advice. What, after all, is the good of a theology which fails us when we need it most? Can a way of thinking about God, life and death be true and yet need to be laid aside at a time of real life crisis? Is there a theology that can genuinely be a means of sustenance for grieving people, which validates their experience of loss but which holds them through it with a sense of hope? On the basis of what we have discovered, the following might be the basic ingredients of such a theology.

Firstly, it must be based on *a biblical view of the creation of human beings*. That is to say, it must abandon once and for all the dualism of Neoplatonic philosophy and affirm afresh the biblical vision of personhood as a psychosomatic unity. As human beings we are body and we are soul, *psyche* and *soma*. We must take seriously the statement in the admittedly anthropomorphic creation story of Genesis, chapter 2, in which the breath of God upon inanimate matter creates, not a soul encased in a body but a 'living soul' inexpressible apart from the body. It is not that body and soul cannot be distinguished conceptually but that they describe two different aspects of human personhood and not two parts of a person which can be separated as we might take the engine out of a car and replace it in another 'body'.

One implication of this is that when our loved ones die we have lost *them* not simply their bodies. Despite the words of Henry Scott Holland they are not 'in the next room' nor anywhere else that we can imagine. They have died and there remains for us the long wait for the resurrection and in the meantime the personal journey of grief in which we painfully adjust to the radical and perhaps unimaginable change to a life without them. This does not, for the Christian raise anxieties for those who have died, as Paul explained to the Thessalonians, because death takes them out of the continuum of time and space until God raises them from the dead. Nevertheless, for those who are left, loss is a reality.

Secondly, a theology which sustains the grieving must be *Christ-centred*. That is, its whole pattern of seeing life, death and resurrection must be centred on the experience of Jesus

Christ. This is insisted on throughout the New Testament and nowhere more emphatically than by Paul. There is no hope beyond death except by analogy with Jesus. The gospel story, while offering positive hope, encourages us to see death as loss. Moreover, both the teaching and experience of Jesus lead us to the conclusion that resurrection life is not simply a continuation of this one but involves radical change – an insight which is repeated by Paul. This is a powerful antidote to sentimentalism. We shall rise as changed people with transformed relationships.

Thirdly, our hope for life after death must rest firmly on faith in *the power of God*. Death is death – and will remain so unless and until God intervenes. The fact that God has, in the gospel, pledged that intervention on the basis of our union with Christ who will come to 'judge the living and the dead', does not make our rising from death 'automatic'. We must not be fooled into thinking of it as a property of our human nature. When the death of our loved ones occurs we who remain are, as much as they, in the hands of God.

Fourthly, the bereaved need a theology which gives validity to *the human experience of suffering* even, perhaps especially, for the Christian. Any view of the Christian life which holds out an ideal of living on a higher plane above the common pains of this life will badly let down the bereaved in their time of need. Rather, the New Testament leads the Christian to expect that his life will, to some extent, reflect the sufferings of Christ as well as the joy of his resurrection. This suffering includes the experience of grief.

It might even be that, like C.S. Lewis, the Christian bereaved will, in their suffering, reach a point which reflects Jesus' sense of abandonment by God. Unless this possibility is allowed – that the Christian might not always feel the reassuring sense of God's presence in times of need – then the feeling of utter isolation that sometimes accompanies grief will be incomprehensible and may lead to a loss of faith. A theology for the grieving must, at all costs, avoid triumphalism.

Finally, in a sense summing up all the other dimensions, a theology for the grieving must base all hope for the future on *the doctrine of resurrection*. The term resurrection means the restoration to life of the whole person. It implies a radical re-creation on the part of God. For this reason even the traditional term 'the resurrection of the body' can be misleading since it seems to apply to only one aspect of personhood and has been used to provide a sort of complement to the idea of the immortality of the soul. Rather, the vision of the New Testament is of a glorified and perfected resurrection of a whole person re-created by God in the image of the risen Christ. This is our hope and only this hope provides an adequate framework of support for those whose need is to accept fully the painful reality of the present in expectation of the glorious consummation which is yet to come.

The real tension in Christian thinking about bereavement does not lie, as is often assumed, between the Christian hope and the painful present. These two are reconciled in the doctrine of resurrection. Rather the tension is between two ways of envisaging the hope of eternal life to which we can give the shorthand titles of *resurrection* and *immortality*, which give rise to two divergent attitudes to grief in the Christian tradition. What I have called the Platonic-Augustinian approach has, from its earliest expression, suppressed grief. The biblical model gives space for grief and is perfectly in tune with the contemporary understanding of what grief is and how it works.

Christians who experience grief and those who in Christ's name want to give support to the bereaved need more than a psychological understanding of the mechanics of the grieving process. We must learn to accept our own and other people's grief, not because it is decreed by experts but because to do so is to be in tune with the deepest insights of the gospel of Jesus Christ.

NOTES

Introduction

1 CRUSE: The National Organisation for the Widowed and their Children offers bereavement counselling and support groups in many parts of the United Kingdom. They can be contacted through their headquarters at Cruse House, 126 Sheen Rd, Richmond, Surrey TW9 1UR.

Chapter 1

1 Gerhard von Rad, *Genesis* (London: S.C.M., 1961), 247.
2 See, for example, von Rad, 246; E.A. Speiser, *Genesis*, The Anchor Bible (New York: Doubleday, 1964), 169; Claus Westermann, *Genesis 12–36: A Commentary* (London: S.P.C.K., 1985), 376. Speiser sums up this view when he speaks of Abraham's weeping as 'a reference to formal rites which has no bearing one way or another on the survivor's personal feelings'. It is interesting to contrast this view with that of Jewish commentators like S.R. Hirsch and Benno Jacob, both survivors of the Holocaust, who see a greater depth of feeling in this passage. See, Samson Raphael Hirsch, *The Pentateuch: Vol 1 Genesis* (New York: Judaica Press, 1971), 381; Benno Jacob, *The First Book of the Bible: Genesis* (New York: K.T.A.V., 1934, abridged 1974), 153. My depiction of Abraham as going into the tent to weep over Sarah is suggested by Hirsch's interpretation of the Hebrew verb as meaning 'coming in' from a public to a private place.
3 Claus Westermann, *Genesis 37–50: A Commentary* (London: S.P.C.K., 1986), 43.
4 Jacob, 256.
5 Hirsch, 353.
6 I have used the word 'principally' because verse 34 — which describes Jacob's adoption of the customary rites of mourning, the tearing of clothes and the wearing of sackcloth — is usually ascribed to another writer E (= Elohistic), so called because he prefers to use the name Elohim for God up to the revelation to Moses at the burning bush. E is said to be an ancient source, but one who is less vivid in his style than the more emotional J.

Skinner, one of the older source critics, sums up the classic view in this way: 'E hardly goes beyond the conventional signs of mourning . . . but J dwells on the inconsolable and life-long sorrow of the bereaved father.' John Skinner, *Genesis, International Critical Commentary* (Edinburgh: T & T Clark, 1910), 448.

 7 See the discussions of the dates of the two narratives in R.P. Gordon, *1 and 2 Samuel* (Sheffield: J.S.O.T. Press, 1984), chapters 6 and 8.

 8 Gordon, 11.

 9 For example, Peter R. Ackroyd, *The Second Book of Samuel*, Cambridge Bible Commentary (Cambridge: Cambridge University Press, 1977), 22.

10 A thorough study of the *qinah* can be found in chapter 8 in 'Mocking Songs & Funeral Dirges,' Otto Eissfeldt, *The Old Testament: An Introduction* (Oxford: Basil Blackwell, 1965), 91–98.

11 Henry P. Smith, *The Books of Samuel*, International Critical Commentary (Edinburgh: T & T Clark, 1912), 258.

12 e.g. William McKane, *I and II Samuel*, Torch Bible Commentaries (London: S.C.M. 1963), 180. John Mauchline, *1 and 2 Samuel*, New Century Bible (London: Oliphants, 1971), 201.

13 Smith, 258.

14 R.P. Gordon, *1 & 2 Samuel: A Commentary* (Exeter: Paternoster, 1986), 259; Ackroyd, 113. This would seem to be confirmed by his later change of clothes but could, of course, be merely an inference from it.

15 S. Goldman, *Samuel* (London: Soncino Press, 1949), 253.

16 J.P. Fokkelman, *Narrative Art and Poetry in the Books of Samuel: Vol 1, King David* (Amsterdam: Van Gorcum, 1981), 275.

17 Fokkelman, 262–263, 275.

Chapter 2

 1 Examples of commentaries which take this position are: Francis Wright Beare, *The Gospel according to Matthew* (Oxford: Basil Blackwell, 1981), 326; David Hill, *The Gospel of Matthew*, New Century Bible (London: Olphants, 1972), 246; Alfred Plummer, *An Exegetical Commentary on the Gospel according to S. Matthew* (London: Robert Scott, 1911), 203; Eduard Schweiser, *The Good News according to Matthew* (London: S.P.C.K., 1976), 319; Robert H. Gundry, *Matthew: a Commentary on his Literary and Theological Art* (Grand Rapids, Eerdmans, 1982), 289.

 2 W.D. Davies, and Dale C. Jr. Allison, *The Gospel according to Saint Matthew*, International Critical Commentary. (Edinburgh: T. & T. Clark, 1991), 485.

 3 Floyd V. Filson, *A Commentary on the Gospel according to St. Matthew* (London: A. & C. Black, 1960), 171.

 4 R.T. France, *The Gospel according to Matthew*, Tyndale New Testament Commentaries. (Leicester, I.V.P., 1985), 286. Le P. M-J. Lagrange, *Evangile selon Saint Matthieu* (Paris: Librairie Victor Le Coffre, 1923), 290.

5 Quoted by B.F. Westcott, *The Gospel according to John* (London: John Murray, 1898), 172.

6 William H. van. Doren, *Gospel of John* (Grand Rapids: Kregel, 1981), 945.

7 J. Ramsey Michaels, *John: New International Biblical Commentary.* (Peabody, Massachusetts: Hendrickson, 1989) C.K. Barrett, *The Gospel according to St. John* (London: S.P.C.K., 1978) *See also Guy, 1963; Westcott, 1989; Bernard, 1928; Schnackenburg, 1980; Plummer, 1910; Hunter, 1965; Carson, 1984; Bultmann, 1971; Raymond E. Brown, The Gospel according to John (i–xii):* Anchor Bible. (New York: Doubleday, 1966), 425, 426.

8 Ray Summers, *Behold the Lamb: an Exposition of the Theological Themes in the Gospel of John* (Nashville: Broadman, 1979) Walter Luthi, *St. John's Gospel* (Edinburgh: Oliver & Boyd, 1960) *See also MacGregor, 1928; Hoskyns, 1947; Sanders & Mastin, 1968; Lagrange, 1936; Edwards, 1954: Tenney, 1948; Lindars, 1972. Barnabas Lindars, although part of the 'grief' camp in his commentary, nevertheless made an interesting suggestion in an article written shortly before his death in 1991. He claimed that John was building upon an original story of exorcism in which the phrase enebrimesato to pneumati* meant 'he rebuked the spirit'; B. Lindars, 'Rebuking the Spirit: A New Analysis of the Lazarus Story: John 11.' *New Testament Studies.* 38, 1992, 89–104. Fascinating as these attempts to reconcile vocabulary are, they become unnecessary when the story is viewed as a narrative of bereavement in which grief and anger are perfectly compatible.

9 van Doren, 945.

10 Ernst Käsemann, *The Testament of Jesus* (London: S.C.M., 1968), 10. See also his discussion of earlier verses in chapter 11 on page 14.

11 Three possible speculations are:

a. Cleopas is to be identified with Clopas, the husband of one of the Marys present at the crucifixion. In this case it would be probable that his companion was his wife: See I. Howard Marshall, *The Gospel of Luke: a Commentary on the Greek Text* (Exeter: Paternoster, 1978), 892f; John Martin Creed, *The Gospel according to St. Luke* (London: Macmillan, 1930, 295.

b. Cleopas is to be identified with a brother of Joseph whose son, Simeon, was later, according to Eusebius, the successor of James as leader of the Jerusalem church: Marshall, 294; E. Earle Ellis, *The Gospel of Luke*, The Century Bible. (London: Nelson, 1966), 276.

c. Origen accepted the above theory and claimed that Cleopas's companion was his son, Simeon. This would have the interesting implication of making the two travellers Jesus' uncle and cousin! H.K. Luce, *The Gospel according to Luke* (Cambridge: Cambridge University Press, 1949), 396.

12 R.B. Rackham, *The Acts of the Apostles*, Westminster Commentaries. (London: Methuen, 1901), 110.

13 F.F. Bruce, *The Acts of the Apostles* (Leicester: Tyndale Press, 1951), 181.

14 A.W.F. Blunt, *The Acts of the Apostles*, Clarendon Bible (Oxford: Oxford University Press, 1923), 164; Everett F. Harrison, *Interpreting Acts: The Expanding Church* (Grand Rapids: Zondervan, 1975), 138; John Stott, *The Message of Acts* (Leicester, I.V.P., 1990), 145.

15 I. Howard Marshall, *The Acts of the Apostles*, Tyndale Commentaries (Leicester: I.V.P., 1980), 151.

16 James Everett Frame, *Epistles of St. Paul to the Thessalonians*, International Critical Commentary (Edinburgh: T & T Clark, 1912), 167.

17 For example, William Neil, *The Epistles of Paul to the Thessalonians*. (London: Methuen, 1957), 92.

18 Quoted by Frame, 166 and Marshall, 119.

Chapter 3

1 Aristeides. *Apology*, XVI:1,6.

2 Aristeides, *Apology*, XV:11,12. Both passages quoted in J. Stevenson, *A New Eusebius* (London, SPCK, 1970).

Chapter 4

1 Biographical details of Plato's life up to this point are found in his *Epistle VII*, which gives us most of the information we have about his life. Although the authorship of this epistle has been challenged, its essential historicity is defended by scholars like Raven. See J.E. Raven, *Plato's Thought in the Making: a Study in the Development of his Metaphysics* (Cambridge: Cambridge University Press, 1965), 19–26.

2 Hugh Tredennick, *The Last Days of Socrates* (London: Penguin, 1969), 43,44. This translation is the source of all references to and quotations from the *Apology* and the *Phaedo*.

3 Raven, 37.

4 Francis Macdonald Cornford, *The Republic of Plato* (Oxford: Oxford University Press, 1945), xxvii.

5 Christopher Gill, 'The Death of Socrates.' *Classical Quarterly*, 23 (1973): 25–28.

6 References to the *Republic* are based on Cornford's translation.

7 Jaroslav Pelikan, *The Shape of Death: Life, Death and Immortality in the Early Fathers* (London: Macmillan, 1962), 80.

8 Pelikan's book gives an excellent summary of the trend of Patristic writing on the subjects of death and the afterlife. Similar accounts can be found in Anton van der Walle, *From Darkness to the Dawn* (London: S.C.M., 1984); John Hick, *Death and Eternal Life* (London: Collins, 1976); Colleen McDannell and Bernard Lang *Heaven: a History* (Yale: Yale University Press, 1988); Simon Tugwell, *Human Immortality and the Redemption of Death.* (London: Darton, Longman & Todd, 1990). Tugwell, however, sees the issue more in terms of *when* resurrection is thought of as taking place than a contrast between resurrection and immorality.

Chapter 5

1 Most of the biographical material concerning Augustine in this chapter is taken from his spiritual autobiography, the *Confessions*. Quotations are from the translation by R.S. Pine-Coffin, (London: Penguin, 1961).

2 Simon Tugwell, *Human Immortality and the Redemption of Death* (London: Darton, Longman and Todd, 1990), 117,118; Peter Brown, *Augustine of Hippo: a Biography* (London: Faber & Faber, 1967), 93.

3 Henry Chadwick, *Augustine* (Oxford: Oxford University Press, 1986), 25.

4 Rod Garner, 'The Thought of St. Augustine.' *Churchman*. 104 (1990): 343.

5 Colleen McDannell and Bernard Lang, *Heaven: a History* (Yale: Yale University Press, 1988), 56,57.

6 Chadwick, 3, 17.

7 Margaret Miles, *Augustine on the Body* (London: Scholar Press, 1979), 99.

8 Romano Guardini, *The Conversion of Augustine* (London: Sands, 1960), 148.

Chapter 6

1 Frank Borkenam, 'The Concept of Death' in Robert Fulton, ed. *Death and Identity* (New York: John Wiley, 1965). Borkenam's preferred name for his third category is 'death-defying'. However, I find this to be an ambiguous term which can easily become confused with the idea of 'death-denying'. I have therefore substituted the term 'death-transcending' which he also uses, although less frequently, to express the same orientation.

2 Roland de Vaux, *Ancient Israel: Its Life and Institutions* (London: Darton, Longman & Todd, 1961), 56.

3 Lloyd R. Sr. Bailey, *Biblical Perspectives on Death* (Philadelphia: Fortress, 1979), 46.

4 Marcus Borg, 'Death as the Teacher of Wisdom,' *Christian Century*, 103 (1986): 203–20.

5 Paul Badham, *Christian Beliefs about Life after Death* (London: S.P.C.K., 1982), 13.

6 See, for example, Bernhard Lang, 'Afterlife: Ancient Israel's Changing Vision of the World Beyond.' *Bible Review*, 4, (1988): 12–32; Badham, chapter 1: 'The Contribution of the Old Testament to the Christian Hope.'

7 Hans Küng, *Eternal Life?* (London: Collins, 1984), 114.

8 Christopher Rowland, *The Open Heaven: a Study of Apocalyptic in Judaism and Early Christianity* (London: S.P.C.K., 1982). For a detailed treatment of the origins of apocalyptic see Paul D. Hanson, *The Dawn of Apocalyptic: The Historical and Sociological Roots of Jewish Apocalyptic Eschatology* (Philadelphia: Fortress, 1975).

9 Bailey, 70.

10 John J. Collins, 'Apocalyptic Eschatology and the Transcendence of

Death,' in Paul D. Hanson, ed. *Visionaries and their Apocalypses* (London, S.P.C.K., 1983), 68. See also D.S. Russell, *Apocalyptic: Ancient and Modern.* (London: S.C.M., 1978), 38.

11 Colleen McDannell, and Bernard Lang, *Heaven: a History* (Yale: Yale University Press, 1988), 29.

12 B.H. Streeter, *Foundations* (London: Macmillan, 1912).

13 G.W.H. Lampe and D.H. McKinnon, *The Resurrection* (London: Mowbray, 1966).

14 Badham, 30–32.

15 Paul and Linda Badham, *Immortality or Extinction?* (London: S.P.C.K., 1982), 22. See also Paul Badham 35–41.

16 Gordon D Fee, *The First Epistle to the Corinthians* (Grand Rapids: Eerdmans, 1987), 715. See also J.M. Ross, 'Does 1 Corinthians 15 Hold Water?' *Irish Biblical Studies*, 11 (1989): 69–72.

17 Brendan Byrne, 'Eschatologies of Resurrection and Destruction: the Ethical Significance of Paul's Dispute with the Corinthians'. *Downside Review*, 104 (1986): 280–98.

18 Karl Barth, *The Resurrection of the Dead* (London: Hodder & Stoughton, 1933), 128.

19 Barth, 196.

20 Barth, 214.

21 For example, C.K. Barrett, *A Commentary on the Second Epistle to the Corinthians* (London: A. & C. Black, 1973), 153; Jean Hering, *The Second Letter of Saint Paul to the Corinthians* (London: Epworth, 1967), 37,38; Ralph Martin, *2 Corinthians* Word Biblical Commentary (Waco, Texas: Word Books, 1986), 105.

22 W.L. Craig, 'Paul's Dilemma in 2 Cor. 5:1–10: A "Catch–22"?'. *New Testament Studies*, 34 (1988): 145–147.

23 Barrett, 151.

24 Rudolf, Bultmann, *The Second Letter to the Corinthians* (Minneapolis: Augsburg Publishing House, 1976), 130. It seems strange to an evangelical writer to find a strong ally in Bultmann! Bultmann's commentary on this passage, however, is outstanding in its clarity. See also T.F. Glasson, '2 Corinthians 5:1–10 Versus Platonism.' *Scottish Journal of Theology*, 43 (1990): 145–155.

25 Oscar Cullmann, *Immortality of the Soul or Resurrection of the Dead?* (London: Epworth Press, 1958).

26 Cullmann, 31.

27 Cullmann, 38.

28 Cullmann, 50–53.

29 Helmut Thielicke, *Living with Death* (Grand Rapids: Eerdmans, 1983), 176,177.

Chapter 7

1 Janice Thomas, 'Some New Directions in the Philosophy of Mind'. *Heythrop Journal*, (1991): 32–37.
2 Michael Paternoster, *Stronger than Death*, (London: S.P.C.K., 1972), 53.
3 John Hick, *Death and Eternal Life*, (London: Collins, 1976), 278.
4 Paul Badham, *Christian Beliefs about Life after Death*, (London: S.P.C.K. 1978), 94.
5 Martin Israel, 'The Nature of Eternal Life: a Mystical Consideration' in Arnold Toynbee, ed. *Man's Concern with Life after Death* (London: Weidenfield and Nicholson, 1976), 157.
6 Ernest Becker, *The Denial of Death*, (New York: Free Press, 1973).
7 Becker, 16,17.
8 Becker, 29.
9 Becker, chapter 3, 25–46, 'The Recasting of some Basic Psychoanalytic Ideas.'
10 Becker, chapters 4 & 5.
11 Becker, 57.
12 Becker, 66.
13 Becker, 203,204.
14 Becker, 204.
15 Ernest Becker, *Psychology Today* (April, 1974): 78.
16 Ray S. Anderson, *Theology, Death and Dying* (Oxford: Basil Blackwell, 1986), 144.
17 Anderson, 143.
18 Anderson, 149.
19 Jessica Mitford, *The American Way of Death* (London: Hutchinson, 1963), 47.
20 Mitford, chapter 5, 'Funerals in England', 169–187.
21 Peter Mullen, *Death be not Proud* (London: Collins/Fount, 1989) 62. The same point is made from a psychological perspective by Beverly Raphael, *The Anatomy of Bereavement* (London: Hutchinson, 1974), 38. See also Tony Walter, 'Secular Funerals'. *Theology*, 92 (1989): 395.
22 Geoffrey Gorer, *Death, Grief and Mourning in Contemporary Britain* (London: Tavistock, 1965).
23 Andrew Walker, *Enemy Territory: The Christian Struggle for the Modern World* (London: Hodder & Stoughton, 1987), 114–121.
24 Lloyd R. Sr. Bailey, *Biblical Perspectives on Death* (Philadelphia: Fortress, 1979), 107,108.
25 Anderson, 155.
26 Anderson, 156.
27 Paul and Linda Badham, *Immortality or Extinction?* (London: S.P.C.K., 1982), 117.
28 Ian Stevenson, *Twenty Cases Suggestive of Reincarnation* (Charlottesville: University Press of Virginia, 1974).
29 See, for example David Cockburn, 'The Evidence for Reincarnation'.

Religious Studies, 27 (1991): 199–207; Raymond Martin, 'Survival of Bodily Death: A Question of Values'. *Religious Studies*, 28 (1992): 165–184; J.J. Macintosh, 'Reincarnation and Relativised Identity'. *Religious Studies*, 25 (1989): 25, 153–165; Harold W. Noonan, 'The Possibility of Reincarnation'. *Religious Studies*, 26 (1990): 483–491; Charles B. Daniels, 'In Defense of Reincarnation'. *Religious Studies*, 26, (1990): 501–504; J.J. Macintosh, 'Reincarnation, Closest Encounters and the Three Card Trick: a Reply to Noonan and Daniels'. *Religious Studies*, 28 (1992): 235–251; Vishal Mangalwadi, 'The Incarnation of the Soul'. *Evangelical Review of Theology*, 15 (1991): 135–147.

30 Hywel D. Lewis, *Persons and Life After Death* (London, Macmillan; 1978), 72.

31 Robert Crookall, *What Happens When you Die?* (London: Colin Smythe, 1978), ix.

32 Shirley Maclaine, *Out on a Limb* (New York: Bantam, 1984).

33 Lewis, chapter 7.

34 Martin Israel, 'The Nature of Eternal Life: a Mystical Consideration', in Arnold Toynbee, ed. *Man's Concern with Life after Death* (London: Weidenfield and Nicholson, 1976), 159. See also H.H. Price, *Essays in the Philosophy of Religion* (Oxford: Clarendon, 1972), 114–115.

35 Raymond A. Moody, *Life after Life* (New York: Bantam, 1984).

36 Simon Tugwell, *Human Immortality and the Redemption of Death* (London: Darton, Longman and Todd, 1990), 72.

37 Christopher Cherry, 'Self, Near-death and Death'. *International Journal for the Philosophy of Religion*, 16 (1984): 11.

38 Tugwell, 16.

Chapter 8

1 E. Lindemann, 'Symptomatology and Management of Acute Grief'. *American Journal of Psychiatry*, 101 (1944): 141–9.

2 E. Lindemann, 'Modifications in the course of ulcerative colitis in relationship to changes in life situations and reaction pattern' 1943. Reprinted in *Beyond Grief: Studies in Crisis Intervention* (New York: Aronson, 1979), 22.

3 Sigmund Freud, 'Mourning and Melancholia' in *The Complete Psychological Works of Sigmund Freud: Vol 14* (London: Hogarth Press, 1917), 243–58.

4 Colin Murray Parkes and Robert S. Weiss, *Recovery from Bereavement* (New York: Basic Books, 1983), 2. Later Freud adapted this theory and claimed that any libidinal withdrawal from a love object is accomplished by identification. See: Sigmund Freud, 'The Ego and the Id', in *The Complete Psychological Works of Sigmund Freud: Vol 19* (London: Hogarth Press, 1923), 12–66.

5 Helene Deutsch, 'Absence of Grief'. *Psychoanalytic Quarterly* 6 (1937): 12–22.

6 Melanie Klein, 'Mourning and its Relation to Manic-Depressive States'. *International Journal of Psycho-Analysis*, 21 (1940): 125–153.

7 John Bowlby, *Attachment and Loss, Vol. 3: Loss: Sadness and Depression* (London: Hogarth Press, 1980), 24.

8 e.g. Bowlby (1980), 31. Parkes and Weiss, 13.

9 Lindemann, (1944), 143.

10 For example Beverly Raphael, 'A Psychiatric Model for Bereavement Counselling', in B.M. Schoenberg, ed. *Bereavement Counselling: A Multi-disciplinary Handbook* (Westport, Connecticut: Greenwood Press, 1980), 147; Lily Pincus, *Death and the Family* (London: Faber, 1975), 258; Joseph H. Smith, 'On the Work of Mourning', in B. M. Schoenberg, ed. *Bereavement: Its Psychosocial Aspects* (New York: Columbia University Press, 1975), 18,19,24; Colin Murray Parkes, *Bereavement: Studies of Grief in Adult Life*, (London: Pelican, 1986), 57,90,95,191; Parkes and Weiss, 155.

11 For example Parkes (1986), 26; Bowlby (1980), 43.

12 For example Parkes (1986), 30,145; Beatrice G. Lipinski, 'Separation Anxiety and Object Loss', in Schoenberg (1980), 3,13,18; R.H. Moos, *Human Adaptation: Coping with Life Crises* (Lexington, Mass; D.C. Heath, 1976), iii; P. Marris, *Loss and Change* (London: Routledge and Kegan Paul, 1974).

13 For example G. Rochlin, *Griefs and Discontents: The Forces of Change* (Boston: Little Brown, 1965), 1; R.S. Weiss, *Loneliness, the Experience of Emotional and Social Isolation* (Cambridge, Mass: M.I.T. Press, 1974); M.R. Feinberg, G. Feinberg and J.J. Tarrant, *Leavetaking: When and How to Say Goodbye* (New York: Simon and Schuster, 1978); Wolfgang and Margaret S. Stroebe, *Bereavement and Health: the Psychological and Physical Consequences of Partner Loss* (Cambridge, Cambridge University Press, 1987), 91–93; Parkes (1986), 145; Lipinski, 10,28.

14 Bowlby (1980), 242.

15 Elisabeth Kübler-Ross, *On Death and Dying* (London: Tavistock, 1970). See also *Living with Death and Dying* (London: Souvenir Press, 1982).

16 Parkes (1986), 27.

17 Bowlby (1980), 83.

18 Bowlby (1980), xiii.

19 Colin Murray Parkes, *Bereavement: Studies of Grief in Adult Life*, (London: Pelican, 1975. New Edition, 1986).

20 John Bowlby, *Attachment and Loss, Vol. 1, Attachment*. (London: Hogarth Press, 1969); *Attachment and Loss, Vol. 2, Separation: Anxiety and Anger*. (London: Hogarth Press, 1973); *Attachment and Loss, Vol. 3, Loss: Sadness and Depression*. (London: Hogarth Press, 1980).

21 Stroebe, 64.

22 Bowlby (1980), 85.

23 For example, Stroebe, 13–15.

24 For example, L. Degner, 'Death in Disaster: Implications for Bereavement'. *Essence*, 1 (1976): 69–77; R.W. Ramsay, and I.A. Happee, 'The Stress of Bereavement: Components and Treatment', in C.P. Speilberger and I.G.

Sarason, eds. *Stress and Anxiety: Vol 4.* (London: John Wiley, 1977), 53–64.

25 Parkes (1986), 84.
26 Beverly Raphael, *The Anatomy of Bereavement* (London: Hutchinson, 1974), 34.
27 Raphael (1974), 35.
28 Parkes (1986), 54, 60.
29 Parkes (1986), 61.
30 John Bowlby, 'Processes of Mourning'. *International Journal of Psycho-Analysis*, 42 (1961): 317–40.
31 Parkes (1986), 72.
32 I. Glick, R.S. Weiss and C.M. Parkes, *The First Year of Bereavement* (New York: Wiley, 1974), 154.
33 W.D. Rees, 'The Bereaved and their Hallucinations', in B.M. Schoenberg, ed. *Bereavement: Its Psychosocial Aspects.* (New York: Columbia University Press, 1975), 67–70. See also W.D. Rees, *The Hallucinatory and Paranormal Reactions of Bereavement*, M.D. Thesis, 1970.
34 P. Marris, *Widows and their Families* (London: Routledge and Kegan Paul, 1958).
35 John Bowlby, *The Making and Breaking of Affectional Bonds* (London: Tavistock, 1979), 53.
36 Raphael (1974), 41–42.
37 Bowlby (1980), 92.
38 Parkes (1986), 96.
39 Bowlby (1980), 93.
40 Raphael (1974), 40.
41 Raphael (1974), 45. See also 216, Raphael (1980), 150.
42 Parkes (1986), 108, 113.
43 Parkes (1986), 111.
44 Parkes and Weiss, 160–1.
45 Parkes and Weiss, 161.

Chapter 9

1 Colin Murray Parkes, *Bereavement: Studies of Grief in Adult Life* (London: Pelican, 1986), 26.
2 John Bowlby, *Attachment and Loss, Vol. 3*, Loss: Sadness and Depression (London: Hogarth Press, 1980), 31.
3 Parkes, 129.
4 Bowlby, 137–138.
5 Bowlby, 138–139.
6 Parkes, 82.
7 Parkes, 90. Bowlby, 87. Raphael, 41.
8 Colin Murray Parkes and Robert S. Weiss, *Recovery from Bereavement* (New York: Basic Books, 1983), 158; Wolfgang and Margaret S. Stroebe, *Bereavement and Health: The Psychological and Physical Conse-*

quences of Partner Loss (Cambridge, Cambridge University Press, 1987), 96.

9 P. Bornstein, et al. 'The Depression of Widowhood after Thirteen Months'. *British Journal of Psychiatry*, 122 (1973), 561–566.

10 I. Glick, R. S. Weiss, and C. M. Parkes, *The First Year of Bereavement* (New York, Wiley, 1974).

11 Parkes, 177.

12 This passage is often found in anthologies for bereaved people, for example Agnes Whitaker, (ed.). *All in the End is Harvest* (London: D. L. T. and CRUSE, 1984).

13 Form the hymn, *In Heavenly Love Abiding* by Anna Laetitia Waring (1823–1910).

14 Beverly Raphael, *The Anatomy of Bereavement* (London: Hutchinson, 1974), 33.

15 Parkes and Weiss, 158.

Chapter 10

1 D. Maddison and B. Raphael, 'Conjugal Bereavement and the Social Network' in Schoenberg, B.M. ed. *Bereavement: Its Psychosocial Aspects*. New York, Columbia University Press, (1975): 30.

2 D. Maddison and W.L. Walker 'Factors Affecting the Outcome of Conjugal Bereavement'. *British Journal of Psychiatry*, 113 (1967): 1057–67; D. Maddison, A. Viola and W.L. Walker 'Further Studies in Bereavement'. *Australia and New Zealand Journal of Psychiatry*, 3 (1969): 63–66.

3 Richard C. Nelson 'Living and Choosing in the Face of Death' in Schoenberg (1980), 135.

4 Parkes (1986), 160–162.

5 Parkes (1986), 180 See also Stroebe, 245.

6 Maddison and Raphael, 37.

7 Raphael (1974), 224.

8 John Corazzini, 'The Theory and Practice of Loss Therapy' in B.M. Schoenberg ed. *Bereavement Counselling: A Multi-disciplinary Handbook* (Westport Connecticut: Greenwood Press, 1980), 75–77.

9 J.W. Worden ,*Grief Counselling and Grief Therapy: A Handbook for the Mental Health Practitioner*, (New York: Springer, 1982), 49.

10 Parkes (1986), 182.

11 I. Glick, R.S. Weiss and C.M. Parkes, *The First Year of Bereavement* (New York: Wiley, 1974).

12 Parkes (1986), 187.

13 Gail M. Giacalone and Eileen McGrath, 'The Child's Concept of Death' in Schoenberg, (1980), 209.

14 Parkes (1986), 188.

15 Parkes (1986), 85.

16 Raphael (1974), 38.

Chapter 11

1 Billy Graham, *Facing Death and the Life After* (Milton Keynes: Word (UK), 1987), 219.
2 Graham, 223.
3 Graham, 240.
4 Graham, 238.
5 Graham, 239.
6 Graham, 26.
7 Graham, 66.
8 Graham, 64.
9 Graham, 204.
10 Graham, 201.
11 Peter Mullen, *Death Be Not Proud* (London: Collins/Fount, 1989).
12 Mullen, 86.
13 Mullen, 124.
14 Mullen, 128.
15 Mullen, 130.
16 Mullen, 148.
17 Mullen, 153.
18 Tony Lake, *Living with Grief* (London: Sheldon/S.P.C.K., 1984).
19 W. Sydney Callaghan, *Good Grief* (London: Collins, 1990), 16.
20 Ian Ainsworth-Smith and Peter Speck, *Letting Go: Caring for the Dying and Bereaved.* (London: S.P.C.K., 1982), 34–36; Jenifer Pardoe, *How Many Times Can You Say Goodbye?: Living with Bereavement* (London: Triangle/S.P.C.K., 1991), 7–9; Susan Wallbank, *Facing Grief: Bereavement and the Young Adult* (Cambridge: Lutterworth, 1991), 8–19.
21 June Cerza Kolf, *When Will I Stop Hurting?: Dealing with a Recent Death* (Grand Rapids: Baker, 1987), 14–26; Jean C. Grigor, *Loss: an Invitation to Grow* (London: Arthur James, 1986), 26–32.
22 Kolf, 45–57; Ainsworth–Smith 55, 56.
23 Ainsworth–Smith 5–13; Pardoe, 10–18; Kolf, 30–36; Grigor, 34–56 et al.; Wallbank, 1992, 47–57; Collick, 28–85.
24 Callaghan, 24, 27, 30, 37, 43, 46, 50, 56.
25 Harold Bauman, *Living Through Grief* (Tring: Lion, 1983).
26 Donald C. Cushenbery and Rita Crossley Cushenbery, *Coping with Life after your Mate Dies* (Grand Rapids: Baker, 1991), 14, 15.
27 Cushenbery, 53.
28 Callaghan, 101–106; Cushenbery, 13–20; Pardoe, 19–31; Wallbank (1991), 24.
29 Ainsworth–Smith, 61–103, 114–128.
30 Callaghan, 101–106.
31 Elizabeth Collick, *Through Grief: The Bereavement Journey* (London: Darton, Longman & Todd/Cruse, 1986), 70–73.
32 Grigor, 132.
33 Wallbank (1991), 24.

34 Susan Wallbank, *The Empty Bed: Bereavement and the Loss of Love* (London: Darton, Longman and Todd, 1992), 73.

35 Pat Wynnejones, *Children, Death and Bereavement* (London: Scripture Union, 1985), e.g. 13, 96–98.

36 Wynnejones, 97.

37 Dodd, Robert V. *When Someone you Love Dies: An Explanation of Death for Children.* (Nashville: Abingdon, 1986), 5.

38 Pardoe, Jenifer *How Many Times Can You Say Goodbye?: Living with Bereavement,* (London: S.P.C.K., (1991), 24.

39 Elaine Storkey, *Losing a Child* (Batavia, Illinois: Lion, 1989), 45, 46.

Chapter 12

1 Roger Lancelyn Green and Walter Hooper, *C.S. Lewis: a Biography* (London: Collins/Fount, 1974), 277.

2 One of the original researchers of the television play *Shadowlands* also wrote a popular biography of C.S. Lewis and Joy Davidman using the same title: Brian Sibley, *Shadowlands: the Story of C.S. Lewis and Joy Davidman* (London: Hodder and Stoughton, 1985).

3 C.S. Lewis, *The Last Battle* (Harmondsworth: Penguin, 1973), 165.

4 This was a favourite theme of Lewis' and one which he elucidates in his religious fantasy, *The Great Divorce.* In this book he adapted an idea from an unknown American science fiction magazine to make everything in heaven so much solider than things on earth that men were ghosts by comparison. The inhabitants of heaven are referred to as 'the solid people'. C.S. Lewis, *The Great Divorce: A Dream* (London: Collins/Fount, 1946), 9, 27, 30.

5 Lewis, *The Last Battle*, 149, 150.

6 C.S. Lewis, *Surprised by Joy: The Shape of my Early Life* (London, Collins/Fount, 1955), 21–23.

7 C.S. Lewis, *Miracles: A Preliminary Study* (London: Collins/Fount, 1947), 149.

8 Lewis, *Miracles*, 150.

9 One reason for doubt about Lewis' resurrectionism is raised by another comment in *The Last Battle*. Here, Professor Kirk exclaims concerning the new heaven which appears on the destruction of Narnia:

> It's all in Plato, all in Plato: bless me what *do* they teach them at these schools (p. 160).

Any idea that Lewis envisages a 'Platonic' heaven is dispelled by the very physical description which follows. Lewis seems to have drawn from Plato not so much a concept of disembodied existence as a sense of solid reality underlying the transience of earthly life. Elsewhere, he contrasts the 'old richly imaginative thought which still survives in Plato' with the 'deathlike but indispensible process of logical analysis' which can be summed up in the saying, 'Heaven is a state of mind' (*Miracles*, p. 135). His biographer and one-time secretary, Walter Hooper sums up: 'He believed that Heaven is the real thing of which earth is an imperfect copy.' Walter Hooper, *Past Watchful Dragons: A Guide to C.S. Lewis's Chronicles of Narnia.* (London: Collins/Fount, 1980), 130.

10 C.S. Lewis, *A Grief Observed* (London: Faber and Faber, 1961), 5.
11 Lewis, *Grief*, 6.
12 Lewis, *Grief*, 7.
13 Lewis, *Grief*, 26.
14 Lewis, *Grief*, 27.
15 Lewis, *Grief*, 15.
16 Lewis, *Grief*, 23.
17 Lewis, *Grief*, 31.
18 Lewis, *Grief*, 32–34.
19 Lewis, *Grief*, 45.
20 Lewis, *Grief*, 49.
21 Lewis, *Grief*, 51.
22 Lewis, *Grief*, 54.
23 Lewis, *Grief*, 56.
24 Lewis, *Grief*, 62.
25 Lewis, *Grief*, 64.
26 Sheldon Vanauken, *A Severe Mercy* (London: Hodder & Stoughton/Spire, 1977, 1989).
27 Vanauken, 35–44.
28 Vanauken, 75–156.
29 Vanauken, 176–178.
30 Vanauken, 179.
31 Vanauken, 187.
32 Vanauken, 194, 195.
33 Vanauken, 222.
34 Vanauken, 231.
35 Vanauken, 209.
36 Freda Baker, *All the Days Ahead: a Testament of Bereavement* (London: Darton, Longman and Todd, 1992), 13, 20, 22.
37 Baker, 27.
38 Baker, 74.
39 Baker, 15; see also 5.
40 Baker, 19; see also: 10, 22, 23, 42, 47, 51, 55.
41 Rosalind Allen, 'What a Beautiful Little Girl That Is' in Ann Warren, ed. *Facing Bereavement* (Crowborough: Highland Books, 1988), 37.
42 Allen, 38.
43 Allen, 41.
44 Robert Dykstra, *She Never Said Goodbye: One Man's Journey through Loss.* (Crowborough: Highland Books, 1990), 19.
45 Dykstra, 119.
46 Dykstra, 69.
47 Dykstra, 19.
48 Dykstra, 104.

49 Dykstra, 106. The adjective 'Cartesian' relates to the philosophy of René Descartes the French philosopher (1596–1650), author of the famous phrase, 'I think therefore I am'. By relating personhood to consciousness, Descartes was able to go on to prove that it was possible for the mind or soul to live independently of the body. This theory was to give an intellectual respectability to the idea of the immortal soul which enabled it not only to survive the sceptical questioning of the Enlightenment period of the eighteenth century but to become one of its leading ideas.
50 Dykstra, 23.
51 Dykstra, 74.
52 Nicolas Wolterstorff, *Lament for a Son* (London: Hodder & Stoughton/Spire, 1989), 8, 9, 26, 28, 34, 38, 54, 67, 81, 91.
53 Wolterstorff, 31.